D0564388

CHICKEN DISHES

HAMLYN
new
COOKERY

CHICKEN DISHES

including recipes for turkey and duck

JENI WRIGHT

First published in Great Britain in 1994
by Hamlyn
an imprint of Reed Consumer Books Limited
Michelin House, 81 Fulham Road, London SW3 6RB
and Auckland, Melbourne, Singapore and Toronto

Copyright © 1994 Reed International Books Limited

ISBN 0 600 58083 0

A CIP catalogue record for this book is available from the British Library

Printed in the UK by Butler and Tanner

ACKNOWLEDGEMENTS
Art Director Jacqui Small
Art Editor Meryl James
Designers Clare White and Barbara Zuniga
Commissioning Editor Nicky Hill
Editors Alexa Stace and Elsa Petersen-Schepelern
Photographer Alan Newnham
Photo Direction Cherry Ramseyer
Step-by-step Photography Jonathan Lovekin
Home Economist Meg Jansz
Stylist Maria Jacques

For my children, Oliver and Sophie

NOTES

Both metric and imperial measurements have been given in all recipes. Use one set of measurements only and not a mixture of both.

Standard level spoon measurements are used in all recipes.
1 tablespoon = one 15 ml spoon
1 teaspoon = one 5 ml spoon

Eggs should be size 3 unless otherwise stated.

Milk should be full fat unless otherwise stated.

Pepper should be freshly ground black pepper unless otherwise stated.

Ovens should be preheated to the specified temperature – if using a fan-assisted oven, follow the manufacturer's instructions for adjusting the time and the temperature.

To test if poultry is cooked, pierce the flesh through the thickest part with a skewer or fork – the juices should run clear, never pink or red.

Do not re-freeze raw poultry which has been previously frozen and thawed. Do not re-freeze a cooked dish which has been previously frozen and thawed.

TURKEY THAWING AND COOKING GUIDE				
WEIGHT	NUMBER OF SERVINGS	THAWING TIME IN A COOL ROOM (BELOW 15°C/60°F)	COOKING TIME AT 190°C (375°F), GAS 5 WITHOUT FOIL	COOKING TIME AT 190°C (375°F), GAS 5 WITH FOIL
1.4-2.25 kg/3-5 lb	4-6	20 hrs	1½-1¾ hrs	1¾-2 hrs
2.75-3.25 kg/6-7 lb	7-9	30 hrs	1¾-2 hrs	2-2¼ hrs
3.5-4 kg/8-9 lb	10-14	36 hrs	2-2½ hrs	2½-2¾ hrs
4.5-5 kg/10-11 lb	15-16	45 hrs	2¼-2¾ hrs	2½-3 hrs
5.5-6 kg/12-13 lb	17-18	48 hrs	2¾-3 hrs	3-3¼ hrs
6.5-8 kg/14-17 lb	19-25	48 hrs	3¼-3½ hrs	3½-3¾ hrs
8.5-12 kg/18-22 lb	26-37	48 hrs	3½-3¾ hrs	3¾-4 hrs
12.5 kg plus/23 lb plus	38 plus	48 hrs	3¾ hrs plus	4¼ hrs plus

CONTENTS

Introduction   6

Quick and Easy   10

Family Meals   38

Around the World   60

Special Occasions   102

Index   128

INTRODUCTION

Poultry meat is quick, versatile and easy to cook, and its quality and flavour are so good it is almost impossible not to make it into a delicious meal, no matter how simple. Chicken and turkey are the two most popular types, with duck reserved for special occasions, and goose eaten mostly at Christmas.

CHICKEN

The best chickens are free-range — more expensive than the battery-farm kind, but full of flavour, succulent and tender. However, if cost is a major consideration, all poultry, free-range or not, is still very good value.

WHOLE CHICKENS

Generally labelled 'oven ready', and weighing anything from 500 g/1 lb to as large as 3.5 kg/7 lb. They can be roasted, pot-roasted, poached or braised. Look for a plump, pliable breast with fairly moist (but not wet) skin, and no broken or dark patches. To check if a whole chicken is cooked, pierce between the leg and thigh with a fork or skewer. The juices should run clear with no trace of pink or red.

POUSSINS

The smallest chickens, no more than 4-6 weeks old, very tender and quick to cook. Cook them whole for 1 person, or spatchcocked for 2.

SPRING CHICKENS

To 12 weeks old, weighing about 1.25 kg/2½ lb, giving 2-3 servings.

LARGER CHICKENS

Older, larger birds are rare these days, and smaller chickens must be substituted when making stocks, soups and broths, and in old recipes calling for 'boiling fowl'.

CHICKEN BREASTS

Bone-in breasts are easy to cook. The bone keeps the meat moist and juicy and prevents overcooking; it slips out easily after cooking.

Suprêmes are boneless chicken breasts with part of the wing bone attached, a speciality cut often used by professional chefs. Any other type of breast may be used instead.

Breasts are also available boneless, with or without skin. The latter is often labelled 'fillet' or 'escalope' if it has been sliced and/or pounded thin.

All breast meat is top-quality lean meat that cooks very quickly — the ultimate convenience food, suitable for pan-frying, sautéeing, grilling, barbecuing, poaching, steaming and stir-frying.

THIGHS AND DRUMSTICKS

Less expensive than breast meat, and better for dishes such as casseroles and stews with long cooking times.

DUCK

Duck is fattier and bonier than chicken or turkey, but is now bred leaner, with a higher proportion of meat to bone.

WHOLE BIRDS

Ducklings (to 8 weeks old) and ducks (over 8 weeks) are best roasted.

JOINTS AND BREASTS

Best for roasting and casseroling. Boneless breasts, or 'magrets', rich and meaty, are available in good butchers and some supermarkets, and make marvellous dinner party fare. Can be roasted, pan-fried, sautéed, grilled and barbecued.

TURKEY

Now available year round, turkey is lean, nutritious and economical. Its rather bland flavour is good with strong-tasting vegetables, herbs and spices to pep up the taste.

WHOLE TURKEYS

Best roasted (see chart on page 4 for oven temperatures and cooking times according to size).

TURKEY JOINTS

Legs, thighs and breasts, bone-in or boneless, sometimes rolled and stuffed, or butter-basted. They are all convenient and good-quality.

BONELESS TURKEY BREAST

Versatile and inexpensive, available thinly sliced as steaks and escalopes, it can be used in any recipe for chicken that calls for boneless breast.

MINCED TURKEY

A low-fat alternative to minced beef.

BONING A WHOLE BIRD

A boned bird makes a wonderful natural casing for a stuffing, joint of meat or another bird. Neat and very easy to carve, this is a special boon at Christmas time, when a large number of people need to be served with hot turkey at the same time. (You could, for instance, bone the turkey on page 126.) Boned, stuffed and rolled birds are also good for buffets and large parties where people help themselves – and they are even easier to carve when served cold.

If just the cavity and breast of the bird are boned, this can be stuffed and reformed back into shape, so that it looks like a conventional bird when cooked (see steps 1-8). You could also bone the whole bird (steps 9-11 on page 8), including the legs and wings, to make a classic ballotine or galantine. A boning knife with a 12-15 cm/5-6 inch blade will make boning easy.

1 Cut off the ends of the legs and wings at the first joints and remove the wishbone as described below.

2 To remove the wishbone, lift back the neck skin from the chicken and cut away the flesh from around the wishbone with the point of a small sharp knife, keeping as close to the bone as possible. Cut out the wishbone and remove any surrounding fat. It is advisable to remove the wishbone in this way even from whole chickens, since it will make the bird easier to carve.

3 Place the chicken with the breast side down on the board, and cut along the backbone, working from tail to neck end.

4 Holding the knife blade angled towards the carcass, carefully scrape the flesh away from the rib cage, working down one side of the bird until the wing is reached.

5 Ease the knife between the ball and socket joint and sever from the rib cage, while keeping it attached to the skin.

6 Continue easing the flesh away from the bone, using small scraping cuts, until you reach the leg joint. Then sever the ball and socket joint in the same way as the wing. Continue until the ridge of the breastbone is reached.

7 Turn the bird around and repeat on the other side.

8 Pull very gently and carefully to separate the breastbone from the skin. You will find that there is no flesh on the chicken at this point, and you must take care not to tear the fragile skin along the ridge of the breastbone, or the bird will split open during cooking. When boning a bird, remember to keep all the bones and trimmings to use later in making stock.

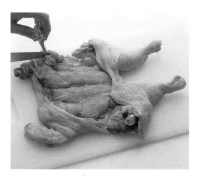

9 Lay the bird flat on the board, with the skin side down. Hold the outside of a wing bone in one hand and, with the knife in the other, carefully scrape the flesh away from the wing bone. Work from top to bottom, and sever all the tendons as you go. Pull out the wing bone. Repeat with the other wing. Push skin and flesh of the wings back inside the carcass to make a neater parcel for stuffing.

10 Hold the inside of one of the leg bones and scrape the flesh away, using a pencil-sharpening action. Sever the tendons as you go, then release the bone when you get to the bottom of the leg. Repeat with the other leg.

11 After boning, the bird is ready to receive the chosen stuffing.

JOINTING A BIRD

The only equipment needed is a large chef's knife which should be very sharp and clean. You can use poultry shears too, but these are not essential.

1 Place breast-side down and cut around the oyster meat on either side of the backbone to expose it.
2 Turn the breast-side up and cut down between the leg and the body. Twist sharply to break the ball and socket joint, then cut to release the leg, keeping the oyster meat attached to the leg. Repeat with the other leg.
3 Cut along both sides of the breastbone, spread the bird open and cut along each side of the backbone (with poultry shears if you have them) and remove.
4 Cut off the knuckle ends of the drumsticks and the wing tips.
5 You now have 4 joints. For 8 joints, cut each diagonally in half. Include some breast meat with each wing. Cut legs through knee joints.

MAKING STOCK

Stock is an essential ingredient in many dishes, especially soups, casseroles and stews. Although it may seem easy to reach for the stock cubes, they rarely have the depth of flavour of a well-made stock and are often very salty. You can buy cartons of freshly made chicken stock at many large supermarkets. These are infinitely better than stock cubes, but there really is no substitute for making your own.

Make a large quantity and freeze in usable amounts (it will keep in the freezer for up to 3 months). To save space, boil it down until reduced, then freeze in ice cube trays to make concentrated stock cubes. Pack them in freezer bags, and when you need chicken stock, drop a frozen cube into hot liquid to dissolve it.

CHICKEN STOCK USING A FRESH BIRD
Boiling fowls, once used for this kind of stock, are rare now. An ordinary oven-ready bird may be substituted.

Do not include the liver when making stock or the finished stock will have a bitter taste.

Use very little salt; seasoning can be adjusted later in the final dish. If too much salt is used in the making of the stock it cannot be reduced later.

Meat left over from stockmaking can be used in cold chicken dishes.

1 Put 1 x 1 kg/2 lb chicken (giblets removed) in a large saucepan with 2.4 litres/4 pints water, add the giblets (except the liver), 1 onion and 1 carrot, both quartered, 1-2 celery sticks, sliced, 1 large bouquet garni, 6 black peppercorns and a pinch of salt. Bring to the boil, skimming the scum as it rises to the surface.

2 Lower the heat, half cover the pan and simmer gently for 3 hours. Skim and top up with water as necessary.

3 Remove the bird and strain stock into a bowl. Blot off any surface fat with paper towels and use the stock immediately, or leave until cold, cover and refrigerate for up to 3 days. Remove any solidified fat.

STOCK USING BONES OR A CARCASS

Always keep leftover bones or carcass. Raw bones and trimmings left after boning or jointing can be used for stock, so too can a carcass leftover after cooking.

1 Break the carcass or raw bones in pieces and put in a large saucepan. Add leftover stuffing and giblets (except the liver), 1.75 litres/3 pints water, 2 celery sticks, sliced, 1 leek and 1 carrot, both quartered lengthways, 1 bouquet garni and a pinch of salt. Bring to the boil and skim off the scum as it rises to the surface.

2 Lower the heat, half cover the pan with a lid and simmer gently for 3 hours, skimming and topping up with water as necessary.

3 Carefully strain the stock through a large sieve or colander into a bowl. Blot off any surface fat with paper towels and use as in previous recipe.

GIBLET STOCK

Giblets make good stock for gravy, but do not include the liver. French cooks chop the liver finely and add it to the pan juices with stock to make a sauce to serve with roast chicken, but if this rather strong flavour is not to your liking, save the liver for another use.

1 Put the giblets from a chicken or turkey (except the liver) in a saucepan with 1.15 litres/2 pints water. Add 1 small onion stuck with 2-3 cloves, 1 carrot, quartered lengthways and 1 celery stick, sliced. Bring to the boil and skim off the scum as it rises to the surface.

2 Lower the heat, cover the pan and simmer gently for 2 hours. Strain the stock into a jug or bowl and proceed as in the recipe on page 8.

POULTRY AND YOUR HEALTH

White meat from poultry is a healthy alternative to red meat, an excellent, economical source of protein, low in fat and cholesterol, and a good source of vitamin B.

1 To reduce fat content, remove the skin before cooking. Skin helps keep poultry moist and succulent during cooking, however, and you may wish to leave it on for cooking but remove it before serving.

2 Raw poultry can contain low levels of salmonella and campylobacter bacteria, responsible for food poisoning. If poultry is stored and handled correctly and cooked thoroughly, bacteria will be rendered harmless. To test if poultry is cooked, pierce the flesh in its thickest part with a skewer or fork – the juices should run clear, never pink or red.

3 Fresh raw poultry should be eaten as soon as possible, or refrigerated immediately and eaten within 2 days or according to packet instructions. Always remove plastic bags and polystyrene trays, place the chicken on a rack over a plate and cover loosely with foil. The rack prevents the bird from sitting in juices that may harbour bacteria. Remove and store giblets separately, unwrapped, in a covered bowl.

4 Completely thaw frozen birds at a cool room temperature before cooking. If any ice crystals remain, birds may not cook thoroughly and any bacteria may not be killed – very important for large birds such as turkeys (see chart on page 4 for thawing times). Never refreeze raw poultry once it has been thawed.

5 Hands, utensils and work surfaces must be scrupulously clean before preparing poultry, and never prepare raw and cooked poultry at the same time. Before cooking, wipe raw poultry with paper towels – very important with the cavities of whole birds which may harbour bacteria. Never stuff the cavity of a bird; stuff the neck end only. If bacteria are present in the bird's juices, these could drip into the stuffing, and the stuffing may prevent the centre of the bird from being thoroughly cooked.

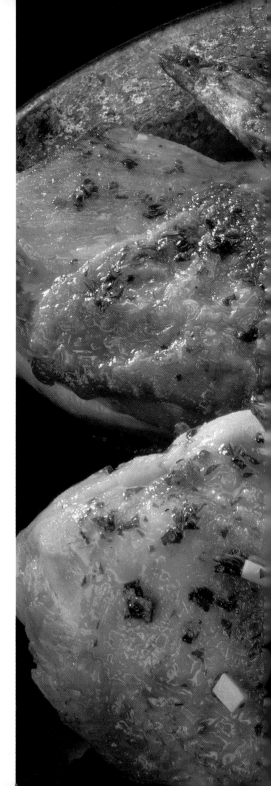

Sauté of Chicken with Garlic, Lemon and Herbs

3 garlic cloves, chopped
4 tablespoons extra-virgin olive oil
4 chicken portions
finely grated zest and juice of 1 lemon
1 tablespoon chopped fresh flat leaf parsley
2 teaspoons chopped fresh tarragon
salt and pepper

TO GARNISH:

lemon slices or twists
fresh herbs

1 Sauté the garlic in the oil until lightly coloured but not browned.

2 Add the chicken in a single layer, season to taste and sauté, turning frequently, for 15-20 minutes until the skin is crisp and golden brown.

3 Lower the heat, cover the pan and continue cooking for 15-20 minutes until the juices run clear when the thickest part of a thigh is pierced with a skewer or fork.

4 Remove the chicken from the pan with a slotted spoon and place on a warmed serving platter.

5 Add the lemon zest and juice to the pan and stir well until sizzling to dislodge any sediment in the bottom of the pan.

6 Remove from the heat and add the herbs and salt and pepper to taste. Stir well to mix, then pour over the chicken. Serve hot, garnished with lemon slices and fresh herbs. A crisp green or mixed salad and French fries would make suitable accompaniments.

Serves 4
Preparation time: 10 minutes
Cooking time: 30-40 minutes

Warm Salad of Chicken, Red Pepper and Lemon

500 g/1 lb skinned chicken breast
   fillets, cut diagonally into thin strips
1 red pepper, cored, deseeded and cut
   lengthways into thin strips
2 tablespoons extra-virgin olive oil
2 Little Gem lettuces, leaves separated
DRESSING:
3 tablespoons extra-virgin olive oil
2 tablespoons lemon juice
1 garlic clove, crushed
1 teaspoon Dijon mustard
salt and pepper

1 Fry the strips of chicken breast and red pepper in the oil, stirring frequently, for 10 minutes or until tender.
2 Whisk the dressing ingredients until thickened. Tear the lettuce leaves and put in a large salad bowl.
3 When the chicken and pepper strips are tender, remove them with a slotted spoon and place on top of the lettuce.
4 Pour the dressing into the pan, increase the heat to high and stir until sizzling. Pour the hot dressing over the salad and toss to combine. Serve immediately, accompanied by good, crusty French bread.

Serves 4
Preparation time: 10 minutes
Cooking time: 10 minutes

Stir-fried Turkey with Pine Nuts and Green Peppers

3 tablespoons rapeseed oil
50 g/2 oz pine nuts
1 onion, sliced finely
2.5 cm/1 inch piece of fresh root
    ginger, crushed
2 green peppers, cored, deseeded and
    cut lengthways into thin strips
500 g/1 lb skinned turkey breast fillets,
    cut diagonally into thin strips
salt and pepper

SAUCE:
2 teaspoons cornflour
2 tablespoons water
2 tablespoons soy sauce
2 tablespoons rice wine or dry sherry
1 tablespoon wine vinegar
1 garlic clove, crushed
1 teaspoon dark soft brown sugar

1 To make the sauce, blend the cornflour and water, add the other sauce ingredients and set aside.
2 Heat 1 tablespoon of the oil in a wok, add the pine nuts and toss for 1-2 minutes until golden brown. Remove and drain on paper towels.

3 Gently stir-fry the onion, ginger and green peppers in the remaining oil for 3-4 minutes until softened but not coloured. Remove and set aside.
4 Stir-fry the turkey for 3-4 minutes until it changes colour on all sides.
5 Whisk the sauce, add to the wok and bring to the boil, stirring until thickened. Add the pepper mixture, toss, then add the pine nuts and toss until the turkey is tender. Season and serve with Chinese noodles.

Serves 4
Preparation time: 15 minutes
Cooking time: 10-15 minutes

Chicken and Sweet Pepper Kebabs

Try to cut the chicken, onion and red pepper into chunks of roughly the same size. This gives the kebabs a neat appearance and helps ensure even cooking.

150 ml/¼ pint natural yogurt
2 tablespoons extra-virgin olive oil
2 garlic cloves, crushed
2 tablespoons chopped fresh coriander
2 teaspoons ground cumin
8 skinned and boned chicken thighs,
   cut into large chunks

1 onion, cut into chunks
1 red pepper, cored, deseeded and cut
   into chunks
1 green pepper, cored, deseeded and
   cut into chunks
salt and pepper

1 Mix the yogurt, oil, garlic, coriander and cumin together in a shallow dish with salt and pepper to taste. Add the cubes of chicken and stir well to mix. Cover and marinate at room temperature for 30-60 minutes.
2 Thread the cubes of chicken on to kebab skewers, alternating them with pieces of onion and red and green pepper.
3 Put the kebabs on the rack of the grill pan. Place under a preheated hot grill and cook, turning frequently, for 20 minutes or until the chicken is tender when pierced with a skewer or fork. Serve hot, on a bed of saffron rice and accompanied by a raita of yogurt, cucumber and chopped fresh coriander.

Serves 4
Preparation time: 15 minutes, plus marinating
Cooking time: 20 minutes

VARIATION

Yakitori Chicken

Yakitori is the Japanese version of kebabs – cook the skewered chicken under the grill, or over hot coals on the barbecue for an authentic charred look.

1 Crush a 5 cm/2 inch piece of root ginger to a paste with 4 garlic cloves and 8 black peppercorns.
2 Place 150 ml/¼ pint Japanese soy sauce (shoyu), 150 m/¼ pint rice wine (sake), 2 tablespoons soft brown sugar and 1 tablespoon oil in a shallow dish. Add the ginger and garlic paste and whisk to combine.
3 Cut 500 g/1 lb skinned chicken breast fillets diagonally into thin strips. Add to the marinade, cover and marinate at room temperature for at least 30 minutes. Meanwhile, soak 16-18 bamboo skewers in warm water.
4 Drain the skewers, then thread the chicken strips on to them, and place under a preheated hot grill for 8-10 minutes until the chicken is tender. Turn the skewers and baste the chicken with the marinade frequently during the cooking time. Serve hot, garnished with spring onion tassels.

Serves 4-6
Preparation time: 15 minutes,
plus marinating
Cooking time: 8-10 minutes

Chilli Chicken

This quick, Indonesian-style curry tastes even better if left to stand overnight and reheated the next day.

3 tablespoons rapeseed oil
1 small onion, chopped finely
2.5 cm/1 inch piece of fresh root
    ginger, chopped finely
2 garlic cloves, crushed
12 skinned and boned chicken thighs,
    cut into bite-sized pieces
2 tablespoons crunchy peanut butter
2-3 tablespoons hot water
2 tablespoons chilli sauce
1-2 teaspoons chilli powder, according
    to taste
1 teaspoon dark soft brown sugar
1 x 400 ml/14 fl oz can coconut milk
¼ teaspoon salt

TO GARNISH:

chilli flowers or rings
chopped roasted peanuts, toasted
    coconut and chopped fresh coriander

1 Heat the oil in a large flameproof casserole, add the onion, ginger and garlic and fry over a gentle heat, stirring, for about 5 minutes until softened but not coloured.

2 Add the chicken, increase the heat to moderate and cook, stirring, for 7-10 minutes, until it changes colour on all sides.

3 Mix the peanut butter and water, then add to the chicken with the chilli sauce, chilli powder and sugar. Stir well to mix for 1-2 minutes.

4 Add the coconut milk and bring to the boil, stirring. Add salt, cover and simmer over a gentle heat, stirring occasionally, for 20 minutes or until the chicken is tender.

5 Serve hot, garnished with chilli flowers or rings and chopped peanuts, toasted coconut and fresh coriander. Steamed or boiled white rice is the only accompaniment you will need with this dish. Serve it with chilled Asian beer.

Serves 4
Preparation time: 10 minutes
Cooking time: about 30 minutes

Sautéed Turkey with Marsala

Use good, dry Marsala, not the over-sweet brands marked 'marsala all'uovo'.

25 g/1 oz butter
1 tablespoon rapeseed oil
4 large skinned turkey escalopes, about 125 g/4 oz each
6 tablespoons Marsala
4 tablespoons water
finely grated zest and juice of 1 lemon
4 tablespoons crème fraîche or double cream
salt and pepper
lemon wedges, to garnish

1 Heat the butter and oil in a large sauté pan, add the turkey in a single layer and sauté for about 5 minutes until golden on all sides.
2 Spoon the Marsala evenly over the turkey, then add the water, lemon zest and juice and salt and pepper to taste. Cover and simmer gently for 15 minutes or until the turkey is tender. Turn it over and baste frequently with the cooking liquid during this time.
3 Stir in the crème fraîche or cream and heat through. Taste and add salt and pepper if necessary. Serve hot, garnished with lemon. Suitable and traditional accompaniments would be polenta fried in butter and olive oil, and a seasonal green vegetable or mixed leaf salad.

Serves 4
Preparation time: 5 minutes
Cooking time: about 20 minutes

Barbecued Chicken Drumsticks

This is the perfect recipe for a summer barbecue – sizzling hot drumsticks with a sweet and sour sauce. They can also be cooked under the grill, allowing a few extra minutes cooking time. If you like, add some red or white wine to the sauce instead of some of the chicken stock. The drumsticks are also excellent served cold for a summer buffet party.

16 chicken drumsticks
300 ml/½ pint Chicken Stock (see
    page 8)
MARINADE:
4 tablespoons tomato ketchup

2 tablespoons Worcestershire sauce
2 tablespoons wine vinegar
2 tablespoons soft brown sugar
2 teaspoons chilli powder
1 teaspoon celery salt

1 Score the chicken drumsticks deeply with a sharp pointed knife, cutting right down as far as the bone.

2 Whisk together all the marinade ingredients in a shallow dish. Add the drumsticks and turn to coat, then cover and marinate in the refrigerator for at least 4 hours, preferably overnight, turning the drumsticks in the marinade occasionally.

3 Put the drumsticks on the grid over hot charcoal on the barbecue. Cook, turning frequently, for about 20 minutes until the chicken is charred on the outside and no longer pink on the inside.

4 Meanwhile, pour the marinade into a saucepan, add the stock and bring to the boil over a moderate heat, stirring. Simmer, stirring occasionally, until the sauce has reduced and thickened slightly.

5 Serve the drumsticks hot, with the barbecue sauce. A nutty rice pilaf is a good accompaniment, together with a colourful mixed pepper salad.

Serves 8
Preparation time: 15 minutes, plus marinating
Cooking time: about 20 minutes

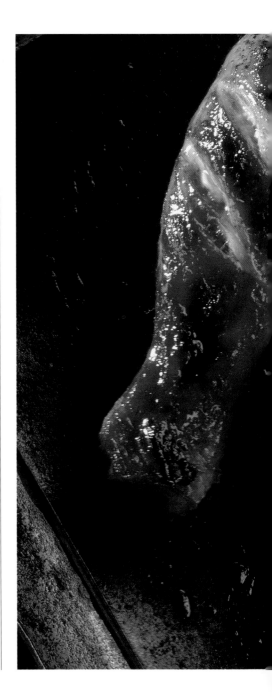

Lemon Chicken

This classic Chinese dish, originally from Hong Kong, appears on the menu in most Chinese restaurants.

1 egg white
2 teaspoons cornflour
500 g/1 lb skinned chicken breast
    fillets, cut diagonally into thin strips
75 ml/3 fl oz rapeseed oil
salt
very finely chopped spring onions or
    strips of lemon zest, to garnish
SAUCE:
2 teaspoons cornflour
6 tablespoons cold Chicken Stock (see
    page 8)
1 garlic clove, crushed
2 tablespoons lemon juice
1 tablespoon soy sauce
2 teaspoons rice wine or dry sherry
1 teaspoon caster sugar
finely grated zest of ½ lemon

1 Whisk the egg white lightly with a fork just to break it up. Add the cornflour and a pinch of salt, and whisk to mix. Add the chicken, turn gently to coat, and set aside.
2 To prepare the sauce, blend the cornflour with 2 tablespoons cold chicken stock in a jug, then blend in the remaining stock and sauce ingredients. Set the sauce aside.
3 Heat a wok or large deep frying pan until hot. Add the oil and heat over a moderate heat until hot but not smoking. Add the strips of chicken, a few at a time, and stir immediately in the oil to prevent them from sticking. Stir-fry for 2-3 minutes until golden and crisp, then remove with a slotted spoon and drain on paper towels.
4 Pour the oil out of the wok. Whisk the sauce, then pour into the wok. Increase the heat to high and bring to the boil, stirring constantly. Simmer for 1-2 minutes, stirring.
5 Lower the heat and return the chicken to the wok. Stir-fry for 2-3 minutes, and check seasoning.
6 Serve immediately, sprinkled with finely chopped spring onions or strips of lemon zest, and accompanied by steamed or boiled white rice and a stir-fried green vegetable.

Serves 3-4
Preparation time: 10 minutes
Cooking time: 15 minutes

Chicken Liver Pâté

Rich and creamy, with the heady aroma and taste of brandy, this pâté is simplicity itself to make. Chicken livers can be bought frozen in tubs from most supermarkets.

375 g/12 oz unsalted butter
2 garlic cloves, crushed
**500 g/1 lb chicken livers, cores
    removed, chopped roughly**
**6-8 tablespoons brandy, according
    to taste**
salt and pepper
parsley sprigs, to garnish

1 Melt 50 g/2 oz of the butter in a large frying pan over moderate heat until foaming. Lower the heat, add the garlic and stir for 2-3 minutes until softened but not coloured.
2 Add the chicken livers, increase the heat to moderate again, and toss vigorously for 5-8 minutes until the livers are browned on the outside, but still pink-tinged in the centre.
3 Pour in the brandy and stir well to mix. Let the mixture bubble for 1-2 minutes, then transfer to a food processor or blender. Cut all but 50 g/2 oz of the remaining butter into pieces and add to the machine. Work the mixture to a smooth pureé and add salt and pepper to taste.
4 Turn the mixture into individual ramekins or a large serving bowl and smooth the surface. Melt the remaining butter in a clean pan, then pour over the surface of the pâté. Leave until cold, then cover and chill in the refrigerator overnight. Serve chilled, garnished with sprigs of parsley and accompanied by triangles of hot wholemeal toast.

Serves 4-6
Preparation time: 20 minutes, plus cooling and chilling
Cooking time: about 10 minutes

Smoked Chicken, Orange and Avocado Salad

The rich, smoky flavour of the chicken is absolutely delicious when combined with this sharp citrus fruit dressing.

1 x 1 kg/2 lb smoked chicken
3 large oranges
50 g/2 oz shelled hazelnuts
2 tablespoons lemon juice
2 teaspoons coarse-grained mustard

1 teaspoon clear honey
100 ml/3½ fl oz hazelnut or
  walnut oil
2 large ripe avocados
salt and pepper

1 Remove the chicken meat from the bones and cut it into neat thin slices, including the skin if you like.
2 Holding the fruit over a bowl, peel and segment 2 of the oranges, taking care not to include any of the membrane and pith.
3 Spread the nuts out on a baking tray and toast under a preheated hot grill for about 5 minutes until browned on all sides. Turn into a clean tea towel and rub off the skins. Roughly chop the nuts.
4 Halve the remaining orange, squeeze the juice and strain into a bowl. Add the lemon juice, mustard, honey and salt and pepper to taste and beat well to mix. Gradually add the oil, beating well after each addition until the dressing emulsifies and thickens.
5 Halve, stone and peel the avocados. Slice the avocado flesh lengthways into neat thin slices.
6 Arrange the smoked chicken and avocado slices on a round serving platter, overlapping the slices slightly so that they form an attractive pattern. Arrange the orange segments in the centre.
7 Whisk the dressing to combine, then drizzle over the salad. Sprinkle with the chopped toasted hazelnuts and serve immediately.

Serves 4-6
Preparation time: 30 minutes

Chicken and Grape Salad

1 Cover a whole chicken with water in a large saucepan with 1 small onion, stuck with 2-3 cloves, 1 carrot and 1 celery stick, chopped roughly, 1 small bunch of fresh tarragon, 1 bay leaf, a few black peppercorns and a pinch of salt. Bring to the boil, cover and simmer for 1 hour or until the bird is tender. Remove the skin and cut the chicken into bite-sized pieces. Reduce the stock by half and set aside.
2 Whip 75 ml/3 fl oz double cream until thick and fold into 150 ml/ ¼ pint mayonnaise. Add the reduced stock, the grated zest and juice of 1 lemon, 1 tablespoon chopped fresh tarragon and salt and pepper to taste. Fold gently to mix.
3 Place the chicken in a large bowl with 125 g/4 oz small seedless green grapes. Spoon over the dressing and mix gently. Cover and chill for at least 2 hours, returning to room temperature before serving.
4 Taste for seasoning and serve on a bed of red and green salad leaves, garnished with fresh tarragon.

Serves 6
Preparation time: 40 minutes, plus cooling and chilling
Cooking time: 1 hour

Devilled Spatchcocked Poussins

2 oven-ready poussins, giblets removed
50 g/2 oz butter, softened
2 tablespoons extra-virgin olive oil
3 tablespoons Dijon mustard
2 shallots or 1 onion, chopped
   very finely
2 garlic cloves, chopped very finely
1 teaspoon dried mixed herbs
salt and pepper
watercress or fresh herbs, to garnish

1 Put a poussin, breast-side down, on a board. Cut along each side of the backbone with poultry shears or a sharp knife and discard.
2 Open out the bird and cut the wishbone in half. Turn the bird over, breast-side up, and push down sharply with the heel of your hand until the breastbone breaks.
3 Trim off the ends of the wings. Make a slit in the skin between the breastbone and leg and tuck the ends of the legs into these slits.
4 Thread skewers across the bird through both wings and legs to keep the bird flat. Repeat with the other poussin, then wipe them both thoroughly with paper towels.
5 Beat the butter, oil, mustard, shallots or onion, garlic, herbs and seasoning until evenly mixed.
6 Put the poussins, skin-side up, on the rack of the grill pan or barbecue and brush with some of the mustard butter. Place under a preheated hot grill, about 7.5 cm/3 inches from the heat, for 25-30 minutes until the juices run clear when the thickest part of a thigh is pierced with a skewer or fork. Turn the poussins once and brush frequently with the mustard butter until it is all used.
7 Cut each poussin in half lengthways with poultry shears or a sharp knife. Place each half on a warmed dinner plate and garnish with watercress or fresh herbs. Serve immediately, with ratatouille for a colourful accompaniment.

Serves 4
Preparation time: 20 minutes
Cooking time: 25-30 minutes

Chicken Waldorf

Chicken or leftover Christmas turkey goes really well in this classic American salad. Add the apples to the mayonnaise immediately after dicing or they will discolour.

125 ml/4 fl oz mayonnaise
about 2 tablespoons lemon juice
375 g/12 oz skinned and boned
    cooked chicken, diced
3 celery sticks, sliced thinly
75 g/3 oz shelled walnuts,
    chopped roughly
50 g/2 oz raisins
2 Red Delicious apples
salt and pepper
crisp lettuce leaves, to serve

1 Put the mayonnaise in a large bowl, add 2 tablespoons lemon juice and stir well to mix.
2 Add the chicken, celery, walnuts and raisins to the mayonnaise and stir well to mix.
3 Core and dice the apples, then add immediately to the salad and stir well to coat. Add salt and pepper to taste, and more lemon juice if liked.
4 Line a salad bowl with lettuce leaves and pile the salad in the centre. Serve at room temperature.

Serves 4
Preparation time: 20 minutes

Pan-fried Chicken Breasts with Sun-dried Tomatoes and Grapes

This recipe has an unusual combination of ingredients, but tastes surprisingly sweet and delicious.

2 tablespoons extra-virgin olive oil
4 part-boned skinned chicken breasts
1 red onion, sliced thinly
2 garlic cloves, crushed
75 g/3 oz sun-dried tomatoes in oil, cut into thin strips
1 tablespoon plain flour
300 ml/½ pint dry white wine
150 ml/¼ pint Chicken Stock (see page 8)
1 teaspoon dried oregano
150 g/5 oz seedless grapes, either black or pink, halved if large
salt and pepper
fresh oregano, to garnish

1 Heat the oil in a large sauté pan, add the chicken, in batches if necessary, and sauté over a moderate heat for 7-10 minutes until golden on all sides. Remove with a slotted spoon and set aside on a plate.

2 Add the onion and garlic to the pan and fry over a gentle heat, stirring frequently, for about 5 minutes until softened but not coloured. Add the sun-dried tomatoes and stir well to combine, then add the flour and cook for 1-2 minutes, stirring. Add the wine, stock, oregano and salt and pepper to taste. Bring to the boil, stirring all the time.

3 Return the chicken breasts to the pan with the juices that have collected on the plate, and stir well to mix. Cover the pan and simmer the chicken over a gentle heat for 20 minutes, or until the chicken is tender when pierced with a skewer or fork. Turn the chicken over and baste with the sauce occasionally during this time.

4 Add the grapes and stir to mix into the sauce. Heat through gently for 1-2 minutes, then taste for seasoning. Serve hot, sprinkled with fresh oregano. Serve with a plain accompaniment, such as new potatoes, to act as a foil for the flavours of the sauce, and follow with a refreshing green salad.

Serves 4
Preparation time: 10 minutes
Cooking time: about 30 minutes

VARIATION

Chicken Paprikash

1 Heat 1½ tablespoons oil and 15 g/½ oz butter in a large flameproof casserole. Sauté 4 skinned chicken portions over a moderate heat for 7-10 minutes until golden. Remove and set aside.

2 Heat 1½ tablespoons oil in the casserole, add 1 large onion, sliced, thinly, 1 garlic clove, crushed, 2 tablespoons sweet Hungarian paprika and 1 large pinch of sugar. Cook gently, stirring frequently, for 10-15 minutes until the onion is soft.

3 Add 1 tablespoon tomato purée and 6 large ripe tomatoes, skinned, deseeded and chopped. Stir well. Add 200 ml/7 fl oz chicken stock and salt and pepper. Bring to the boil, stirring. Add the chicken and its juices, cover and simmer over a gentle heat, stirring occasionally, for 40 minutes or until the chicken is cooked. Check the seasoning.

4 Serve hot, topped with spoonfuls of soured cream. Buttered noodles tossed in caraway or poppy seeds are the traditional accompaniment.

Serves 4
Preparation time: 30 minutes
Cooking time: about 50 minutes

Tex-Mex Chicken with Salsa

6 large chicken breast fillets
6 tablespoons extra-virgin olive oil
finely grated zest and juice of 2 limes
¾ teaspoon ground cumin

SALSA:

500 g/1 lb ripe tomatoes, skinned,
    deseeded and chopped finely
1 small onion, chopped very finely
2 garlic cloves, crushed
1 hot green chilli, deseeded and
    chopped very finely
3 tablespoons extra-virgin olive oil
2 teaspoons wine vinegar
juice of 1 lime
¼ teaspoon salt

1 Score each chicken breast diagonally in several places with a sharp knife. Whisk together the olive oil, lime zest and juice and the cumin. Brush over the chicken, working it into the incisions in the flesh. Cover and marinate for about 1 hour.

2 To make the salsa, put all the ingredients in a bowl and stir well to mix. Cover and chill in the refrigerator until serving time.

3 Put the chicken on the grid over hot charcoal on the barbecue. Reserve the marinade. Cook for 5-7 minutes on each side or until the chicken feels tender when pierced with a skewer or fork, brushing frequently with the reserved marinade.

4 Slice the chicken diagonally, along the lines of the first incisions. Arrange alongside the salsa on warmed plates. Serve immediately. Avocado slices and corn tortillas are the traditional accompaniments.

Serves 6
Preparation time: 15 minutes,
plus marinating
Cooking time: 10-15 minutes

Warm Chicken Liver Salad with Honey and Mustard Dressing

For convenience, use the ready-prepared salad leaves available from most large supermarkets.

25 g/1 oz butter
250 g/8 oz chicken livers, cores removed, cut into bite-sized pieces
250 g/8 oz mixed salad leaves (radicchio, frisée, oak leaf lettuce and rocket)
salt and pepper
DRESSING:
3 tablespoons extra-virgin olive oil
1 tablespoon raspberry vinegar
2 teaspoons clear honey
1 teaspoon coarse-grained mustard
salt and pepper

1 First make the dressing. Put all the ingredients in a large salad bowl with salt and pepper to taste. Whisk with a fork until evenly combined and thickened, then adjust the seasoning to taste. Set aside.
2 Melt the butter in a frying pan over a moderate heat until foaming. Add the chicken livers and toss vigorously for 5-8 minutes until the livers are browned on the outside, but still tinged with pink in the centre. Season to taste with salt and pepper.
3 Quickly toss the salad leaves in the dressing, then arrange on individual plates. Spoon the chicken livers and cooking juices over the top. Serve immediately as a first course or light lunch dish, with hot, crisp bread.

Serves 4
Preparation time: 10 minutes
Cooking time: 5-8 minutes

Chicken with Cream Cheese, Garlic and Herbs

If you use Boursin cheese with garlic and herbs already mixed in, this dish will be even quicker to prepare.

4 large boned chicken breasts
125 g/4 oz cream cheese or low-fat
   soft cheese
3 tablespoons finely chopped fresh
   mixed fresh herbs (such as tarragon,
   dill, parsley, chervil) or 2 teaspoons
   dried mixed herbs

1-2 garlic cloves, crushed
15 g/½ oz butter
salt and pepper
fresh herbs, to garnish

1 Insert your fingers between the skin and the flesh of each chicken breast to make a 'pocket'.
2 Put the cheese in a bowl with the herbs, garlic and salt and pepper to taste. Beat well to mix.
3 Push the cheese mixture into the pockets in the chicken breasts, dividing it equally between them. Smooth the skin over the cheese to make it as compact as possible.
4 Melt the butter in a small saucepan, then use to brush a baking dish. Arrange the chicken breasts in a single layer in the dish, then brush with the remaining butter and sprinkle with salt and pepper to taste.
5 Place in a preheated oven, 220°C (425°F), Gas Mark 7 for 20 minutes or until the chicken is tender when pierced with a skewer or fork. Serve hot, cut diagonally into slices if liked, garnished with fresh herbs. New potatoes, and a salad of thinly sliced cucumber and fresh dill with an oil and vinegar dressing would make good accompaniments.

Serves 4
Preparation time: 15 minutes
Cooking time: 20 minutes
Oven temperature: 220°C (425°F), Gas Mark 7

VARIATION

Swiss Chicken

Another good chicken-and-cheese recipe.

1 In a large sauté pan, gently sauté 2 carrots, 2 courgettes and 1 celery stick, all sliced into matchsticks, in 25 g/1 oz butter for 2-3 minutes.
2 Place 4 large skinned chicken breast fillets on top of the vegetables. Add 125 ml/4 fl oz dry white wine and 125 ml/4 fl oz chicken stock, bring to the boil, cover and simmer for 10 minutes.
3 Drain and reserve the cooking liquid and boil until reduced by half. Pour in 250 ml/8 fl oz double cream, and simmer for about 5 minutes, stirring, until thickened. Meanwhile, continue cooking the chicken and vegetables for another 10 minutes more.
4 Lightly whisk 2 egg yolks in a bowl with a spoonful of the cream and stock mixture, then stir into the cream and stock mixture in the pan. Add 75 g/3 oz grated Gruyère cheese. Heat gently, stirring, until the cheese is melted and the sauce is thick and smooth.
5. Serve the chicken pieces coated with the cheese sauce, with the vegetables arranged on top.

Serves 4
Preparation time: 20 minutes
Cooking time: 30-35 minutes

Chicken and Mangetout in Black Bean Sauce

Presentation is all important in Chinese cooking, so cut the chicken and vegetables into thin strips the same length as the mangetout.

3 tablespoons rapeseed oil

1 red pepper, cored, deseeded and cut lengthways into thin strips

2 celery sticks, cut into very thin matchstick strips

2.5 cm/1 inch piece of fresh root ginger, cut into very thin matchstick strips

2 garlic cloves, crushed

125 g/4 oz small mangetout

500 g/1 lb skinned chicken breast fillets, cut diagonally into thin strips

4 tablespoons black bean sauce

4 tablespoons water

salt and pepper

1 Heat 2 tablespoons of the oil in a wok or large, deep frying pan until hot but not smoking. Add the red pepper, celery, ginger and garlic and stir-fry over a gentle heat for 3-4 minutes until the vegetables are just softened but not coloured.

2 Add the mangetout and stir-fry for a further minute, taking care that they are still crisp and crunchy. Remove all the vegetables with a slotted spoon and set aside.

3 Heat the remaining oil in the wok, add the chicken and stir-fry over a moderate heat for 3-4 minutes until it changes colour on all sides.

4 Add the black bean sauce and the water and stir-fry for a further 2-3 minutes until the chicken is tender when pierced with a skewer or fork.

5 Return the stir-fried vegetables to the wok and toss for 1-2 minutes until all of the ingredients are evenly mixed and piping hot. Add salt and pepper to taste. Serve immediately, with Chinese egg noodles or steamed or boiled white rice.

Serves 4

Preparation time: 10 minutes

Cooking time: 10-15 minutes

Penne with Chicken and Pesto

2 tablespoons extra-virgin olive oil
250 g/8 oz penne or other pasta
375 g/12 oz skinned chicken breast fillets, cut diagonally into thin strips
3 tablespoons pesto (basil sauce)
4-6 tablespoons double cream
salt and pepper

TO GARNISH:
freshly grated Parmesan cheese
basil leaves

1 Add 1 tablespoon of the oil and ½ teaspoon salt to a large saucepan of boiling water. Add the penne or other pasta shapes. Boil, uncovered, over a moderate heat for about 10 minutes, or according to packet instructions, until *al dente*.

2 Meanwhile, heat a wok or large deep frying pan over a moderate heat until hot, add the remaining oil and heat until hot but not smoking. Add the chicken and stir-fry for 3-4 minutes until it changes colour on all sides.

3 Add the pesto and stir-fry for 2-3 minutes until the chicken is tender.

4 Drain the pasta well, add to the chicken mixture and toss over a high heat until evenly mixed with the chicken and pesto. Add the cream and salt and pepper to taste and toss well to mix. Serve in warmed bowls or soup plates, and garnish with grated Parmesan and basil.

Serves 3-4
Preparation time: 5 minutes
Cooking time: 10-15 minutes

Quick Stir-fried Duck with Pineapple

The richness of duck is perfectly complemented by the sharp sweetness of pineapple. Omit the chilli powder if you prefer a milder dish, but it does give a pleasant kick to the overall flavour of the stir-fry. Always take care when adding chilli powder because some varieties are very hot indeed. Chinese five-spice powder is available in small jars in the spice section of most large supermarkets, and is used in the stir-fry variation using chicken (see at right).

2 tablespoons rapeseed oil

4 duck breast fillets, each about
175 g/6 oz, skin and fat removed,
cut diagonally into thin strips

¼-½ teaspoon chilli powder, according
to taste

2 tablespoons soy sauce

2 tablespoons sweet sherry

1 x 250 g/8 oz can pineapple chunks
in natural juice, drained, with
juice reserved

4-6 spring onions, cut diagonally into
5 cm/2 inch lengths

salt and pepper

1 Heat a wok or a large deep frying pan over a moderate heat until hot. Add the oil and heat until hot but not smoking. Add the duck and stir-fry for about 5 minutes until it changes colour on all sides.
2 Sprinkle in the chilli powder and stir-fry for 1 minute. Add the soy sauce, sherry, pineapple juice, and salt and pepper to taste.
3 Stir-fry for about 5 minutes or until the duck is tender when pierced with a skewer or fork, adding the pineapple chunks and spring onions for the last minute or so to heat through.
4 Serve immediately. Suitable accompaniments would be white and wild rice mixed together, with a side dish of steamed mangetout or broccoli.

Serves 3-4
Preparation time: about 10 minutes
Cooking time: about 10 minutes

VARIATION

Five-spice Chicken with Cashew Nuts

1 Blend 1 teaspoon cornflour with 2 tablespoons each of water and rice wine or dry sherry. Stir in 2 tablespoons soy sauce and 2 teaspoons wine or cider vinegar, followed by 1 teaspoon clear honey and ¼ teaspoon five-spice powder. Set aside.
2 Heat 1 tablespoon rapeseed oil in a wok, add 75 g/3 oz shelled, unsalted cashews and the white parts of 6-8 spring onions, sliced diagonally into 5 cm/2 inch lengths. Stir-fry for 1 minute until the cashews change colour. Remove and drain on paper towels.
3 Heat 2 tablespoons rapeseed oil in the wok, add 500 g/1 lb skinned chicken breast fillets, cut diagonally into thin strips, and 1 garlic clove, crushed. Stir-fry as in the main recipe.
4 Whisk the sauce and pour into the wok. Stir-fry until the chicken is tender and the sauce is thick and glossy. Return the cashew and spring onion mixture to the wok, with the green tops of the spring onions. Stir-fry for 30 seconds, taste for seasoning and add more soy sauce if liked. Serve immediately.

Serves 4
Preparation time: 10 minutes
Cooking time: about 10 minutes

Soy Duck

This sweet and spicy marinade gives duck a Chinese flavour.

4 duck breast fillets, each about 175 g/6 oz
300 ml /½ pint water
spring onion tassels, to garnish
MARINADE:
3 tablespoons rice wine or dry sherry
2 tablespoons soy sauce
1 tablespoon clear honey
1 tablespoon tomato purée
2 garlic cloves, crushed

1 Score the duck skin and fat with a sharp knife, making several diagonal incisions in each fillet.
2 Put the marinade ingredients in a shallow dish large enough to hold the duck breasts in a single layer.
3 Whisk the marinade ingredients together until evenly combined, then put the duck breasts, skin-side up, in the dish and spoon over the marinade. Cover and marinate in the refrigerator for at least 4 hours, preferably overnight.
4 When ready to cook, lift the duck breasts out of the marinade and place, skin-side down, in a single layer in a large cast-iron, heavy-based frying pan. Whisk the water into the marinade left in the dish and set aside.
5 Cook the duck breasts over a gentle to moderate heat for about 5 minutes until the fat runs and the skin is golden brown. During this stage of the cooking, press the duck breasts down hard with a fish slice to keep them as flat as possible. The honey in the marinade has a tendency to catch at this point, so do take care that the duck skin does not burn.
6 Drain off all the fat from the pan and turn the duck breasts so they are skin-side up. Pour over the reserved marinade, then cook over a gentle heat, basting frequently with the cooking juices, for 20 minutes or until the duck is tender when pierced with a skewer or fork.
7 Remove the duck from the cooking juices and cut diagonally into slices, following the lines of the incisions in the skin. Arrange the slices on warmed dinner plates, spoon the cooking juices over the duck and garnish with spring onion tassels. Serve hot, with buttered noodles or steamed or boiled rice and a crisp and refreshing Iceberg lettuce salad.

Serves 4
Preparation time: 10 minutes, plus marinating
Cooking time: 25 minutes

Chop Suey

Chop suey means 'bits and pieces' and Chinese cooks use whatever leftover ingredients they have to hand. Real Chinese roast chicken is used in this recipe. Available from large supermarkets, it gives an authentic oriental flavour.

2 tablespoons rapeseed oil
1 onion, sliced thinly
1 garlic clove, crushed
3 carrots, cut into very thin
   matchstick strips
125 g/4 oz button mushrooms,
   sliced thinly
1 x 125 g/4 oz packet frozen mixed
   vegetables (peas, sweetcorn
   and peppers)
about 250-375 g/8-12 oz skinned
   and boned Chinese roast chicken, or
   cooked chicken or turkey,
   cut into strips
250 g/8 oz bean sprouts
salt and pepper
SAUCE:
2 teaspoons cornflour
4 tablespoons water
2 tablespoons soy sauce
1 tablespoon rice wine or dry sherry
1 tablespoon wine vinegar
2 teaspoons soft brown sugar

1 First make the sauce. Blend the cornflour with the water in a jug, then stir in the soy sauce, the rice wine or dry sherry, the wine vinegar and the soft brown sugar. Set aside.

2 Heat a wok or large deep frying pan over a moderate heat, add the rapeseed oil and heat until hot but not smoking. Add the onion and garlic and stir-fry over a gentle heat for 1-2 minutes until softened but not coloured, then add the carrots and stir-fry for 5 minutes longer.
3 Add the mushrooms and frozen mixed vegetables, increase the heat to high and toss vigorously for 2-3 minutes until the vegetables are defrosted.
4 Add the chicken and bean sprouts and stir well to mix. Whisk the sauce again to combine thoroughly and

pour it into the wok. Toss vigorously until the sauce has thickened and coated the chicken and vegetables. Taste and add salt and pepper if necessary. Serve immediately, with Chinese noodles or steamed or boiled rice.

Serves 3-4
Preparation time: 20 minutes
Cooking time: about 10 minutes

French Roast Chicken

Roast garlic 'flowers' with the chicken, allowing 1 garlic head per person. Slice off the tops, place cut-side up in a single layer in an oiled ovenproof dish and drizzle 1 tablespoon extra-virgin olive oil over each. Place in the oven for the last 50 minutes of the roasting time and baste after 25 minutes. To eat, squeeze the softened flesh out of the skins.

1 x 2 kg/4 lb oven-ready chicken, giblets removed
1 bunch of fresh mixed herbs (such as tarragon, parsley, rosemary, thyme)
1 garlic clove, quartered
75 g/3 oz butter
300 ml/½ pint Giblet Stock (see page 9)
125 ml/4 fl oz dry white wine
salt and pepper

1 Wash and dry the chicken cavity, insert the herbs and garlic and season to taste. Truss the chicken, spread it with butter and sprinkle with pepper. Place on its side in a close-fitting roasting tin. Pour half the stock around it.
2 Roast in a preheated oven, 200°C (400°F), Gas Mark 6, for 1 hour 40 minutes or until tender. Turn over every 25 minutes, first on its breast, then on its other side, and finally on its back. Baste well each time it is turned.
3 Remove the chicken, cover with foil and set aside to rest in a warm place.
4 Pour off most of the fat, set the tin on top of the stove and add the wine and remaining stock. Bring to the boil, scraping the sediment from the tin. Simmer, stirring, until the sauce is reduced and thickened. Check seasoning.
5 Discard the trussing string, carve the chicken and arrange on warmed dinner plates with the sauce spooned over.

Serves 4
Preparation time: 20 minutes
Cooking time: 1 hour 40 minutes
Oven temperature: 200°C (400°F), Gas Mark 6

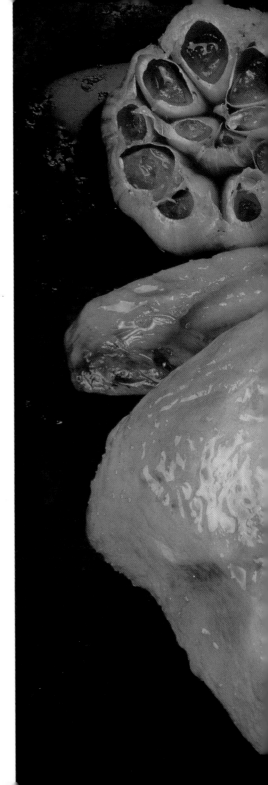

Curried Turkey Meatballs

Use fresh turkey, or leftover roast turkey.

500 g/1 lb minced turkey
1 tablespoon garam masala
1 teaspoon chilli powder
1 teaspoon ground ginger
2 garlic cloves, crushed
1 egg, beaten
2 tablespoons rapeseed oil
1 onion, chopped finely
3 tablespoons curry paste
1 tablespoon tomato purée
450 ml/¾ pint Turkey Stock
**   (see page 8) or water**
salt
a sprig of mint, to garnish

1 Mix the turkey with garam masala, chilli powder, ginger, half the garlic, beaten egg and ½ teaspoon salt (the mixture will be moist and sticky). With wet hands, shape into 16-20 small balls. Chill for at least 1 hour.
2 Heat the oil in a non-stick frying pan. Add half the meatballs in a single layer and fry over a moderate heat for about 5 minutes until browned on all sides. Shake the pan constantly during this time to turn the meatballs over so that they colour evenly. Transfer to a flameproof casserole with a slotted spoon. Repeat with the remaining meatballs, arranging them in a single layer in the casserole when browned.
3 Add the onion and remaining garlic to the frying pan and fry over a gentle heat, stirring frequently, for

about 5 minutes until softened. Add the curry paste and tomato purée and stir well to mix. Gradually pour in the stock or water, stirring vigorously to combine with the onion mixture. Add ½ teaspoon salt and bring to the boil, stirring all the time.
4 Pour the sauce over the meatballs and shake the casserole so the sauce covers them evenly. Cover and cook over a gentle heat for 20 minutes, shaking the pan frequently so that the meatballs are always covered in sauce. Serve hot, garnished with mint, on a bed of saffron or turmeric rice, accompanied by a cucumber raita.

Serves 4-6
Preparation time: 30 minutes
Cooking time: 20 minutes

Waterzooi

This 'meal-in-a-bowl' chicken and leek soup comes originally from Belgium, hence its strange-sounding name. It is rich and delicious with its last-minute addition of egg and cream, and the chicken stock cubes give it an even fuller flavour, but you can leave out these ingredients if you prefer a plainer soup.

1 x 2 kg/4 lb oven-ready chicken, giblets removed
thinly pared zest of 1 lemon
1 onion, sliced thinly
3 carrots, sliced thickly
2 celery sticks, sliced thickly
2.1-2.4 litres/3½-4 pints water
1 large bouquet garni
3 medium leeks, trimmed, cleaned and sliced thickly
salt and pepper

TO FINISH:

1-2 chicken stock cubes, according to taste
1 egg yolk
4 tablespoons double cream
finely grated zest of 1 lemon
2 tablespoons finely chopped fresh parsley

1 Put the chicken in a large saucepan and add the lemon zest, onion, carrots and celery. Pour in the water to cover, then add the bouquet garni and salt and pepper to taste. Bring to the boil over a moderate heat. Lower the heat, cover and simmer for 1½ hours or until the chicken is tender and the juices run clear when the thickest part of a thigh is pierced with a skewer or fork.

2 Lift the chicken out of the liquid and leave until cool enough to handle. Remove and discard the lemon zest and bouquet garni.

3 Add the leeks to the liquid in the pan and simmer, uncovered, over a moderate heat for 10 minutes or until just tender. Meanwhile, remove the chicken meat from the bones, and discard all skin and fat. Cut the chicken into bite-sized pieces.

4 Crumble the stock cubes in a bowl, add the egg yolk and cream and stir well to mix. Add a few spoonfuls of the hot soup liquid and stir well again, then whisk this mixture gradually back into the soup. Add the chicken and simmer over a gentle heat, stirring constantly, for about 5 minutes until the chicken is heated through and the soup has thickened slightly.

5 Remove the soup from the heat and stir in the lemon zest and parsley. Taste for seasoning. Serve hot as a supper or lunch dish, with a warm baguette or hot garlic bread.

Serves 4-6
Preparation time: 20 minutes
Cooking time: about 1¾ hours

Chicken Cannelloni

You could use petits pois instead of the sweetcorn kernels, or half and half for a more colourful effect. Be sure to buy the 'no pre-cooking required' kind of cannelloni.

50 g/2 oz frozen sweetcorn kernels
50 g/2 oz butter
50 g/2 oz plain flour
700 ml/24 fl oz milk
175 g/6 oz Cheddar cheese, grated
250 g/8 oz skinned and boned
   cooked chicken, shredded

¼ teaspoon freshly grated nutmeg
12 cannelloni tubes
good pinch of paprika
salt and pepper

1 Cook the frozen sweetcorn kernels in salted boiling water for 3 minutes, or according to packet instructions, until tender. Drain well and set aside.
2 Melt the butter in a saucepan, sprinkle in the flour and stir over a moderate heat for 1-2 minutes. Remove from the heat and add half the milk a little at a time, beating vigorously after each addition.
3 Return the pan to the heat and bring to the boil, stirring all the time. Lower the heat and simmer, stirring, for about 5 minutes until very thick and smooth. Remove the pan from the heat and transfer half the sauce to a bowl.
4 Add one-third of the grated Cheddar to the sauce in the bowl with the chicken, sweetcorn, half the nutmeg and salt and pepper to taste. Stir well.
5 Over a moderate heat, gradually beat the remaining milk into the sauce in the pan, bring to the boil and simmer, stirring, for 5 minutes, until thick and smooth. Add half the remaining cheese, the remaining nutmeg, and salt and pepper to taste. Stir until the cheese melts. Remove from the heat, then pour about one-third of the sauce into a large ovenproof dish. Spread evenly.
6 With a teaspoon, fill the cannelloni tubes with the chicken mixture. Place the tubes in a single layer in the dish as you fill them.
7 Pour over the remaining sauce and sprinkle with the remaining cheese and the paprika. Place in a preheated oven, 190°C (375°F), Gas Mark 5 for 30-35 minutes until bubbling and golden. Serve hot, with a mixed salad.

Serves 4-6
Preparation time: 30 minutes
Cooking time: 30-35 minutes
Oven temperature: 190°C (375°F), Gas Mark 5

VARIATION

Chicken Pasticciata

Another good pasta recipe. This one, smooth and creamy, is popular with children.

1 Cook 175 g/6 oz penne or other pasta shapes, until *al dente*. Make a white sauce with 25 g/1 oz each butter and flour and 600 ml/1 pint milk. Remove from the heat, add 125 g/4 oz mozzarella, diced, 20 g/¾ oz grated Parmesan, a pinch of nutmeg, salt and pepper.
2 Drain the pasta and mix with 250 g/8 oz skinned and boned cooked chicken, cut into thin strips. Mix with two-thirds of the cheese sauce.
3 Spread the mixture in a baking dish. Mix 2 beaten eggs into the remaining sauce and pour over the top. Sprinkle with 20 g/¾ oz grated Parmesan and bake in a preheated oven, 190°C (375°F), Gas Mark 5 for 20 minutes until bubbling and golden. Serve with a crisp crunchy salad.

Serves 4
Preparation time: 30 minutes
Cooking time: 20 minutes
Oven temperature: 190°C (375°F), Gas Mark 5

Sunday Roast Chicken

The onion quarters and bacon rashers flavour the chicken, help make the meat moist, and give extra flavour to the gravy.

1 x 2 kg/4 lb oven-ready chicken, giblets removed
1 small onion, quartered
1-2 tablespoons rapeseed oil
6 streaky bacon rashers
1 tablespoon plain flour
450 ml/¾ pint Giblet Stock (see page 9) or water
2-3 tablespoons dry or medium sherry
salt and pepper

1 Wash the cavity of the chicken and dry thoroughly with paper towels. Put the onion quarters inside the chicken cavity, season to taste, and truss the chicken with string.
2 Put the chicken on a rack in a roasting tin into which it just fits. Brush the bird all over with the oil, sprinkle with pepper and lay the bacon rashers on top.
3 Roast in a preheated oven, 190°C (375°F), Gas Mark 5 for 2 hours, or until the juices run clear when the thickest part of a thigh is pierced with a skewer or fork. Baste several times during roasting, and cover with foil if the bacon and top of the chicken become too brown.
4 Lift the chicken out of the tin, then cover the bird tightly with foil and set aside to rest in a warm place while making the gravy.
5 Pour off all but about 1 tablespoon of the cooking juices and set the tin on top of the stove. Sprinkle in the flour and cook over a gentle heat, stirring, for 1-2 minutes until browned. Gradually stir in the stock or water and bring to the boil over a moderate heat, stirring all the time. Lower the heat, add the sherry and salt and pepper to taste, then simmer, stirring, for a few minutes or so until the gravy thickens. Adjust the seasoning to taste, then pour into a warmed gravy boat.
6 Remove the trussing string from the chicken and discard. Put the chicken on a warmed serving platter and carve at the table. Hand the gravy separately in a sauce boat. Serve with bread sauce, Brussels sprouts, bacon rolls and chipolata sausages.

Serves 4
Preparation time: 20 minutes
Cooking time: about 2 hours
Oven temperature: 190°C (375°F), Gas Mark 5

Chicken and Lemon Croquettes

25 g/1 oz butter
2 tablespoons plain flour
150 ml/¼ pint milk
250 g/8 oz skinned and boned cooked
  chicken, chopped finely
2-3 teaspoons finely chopped fresh
  tarragon or parsley
finely grated zest of 2 lemons
1 egg, beaten
about 75 g/3 oz fine dried
  breadcrumbs
2 tablespoons rapeseed oil
salt and pepper
TO SERVE:
lemon wedges
tarragon or parsley sprigs

1 Melt the butter in a saucepan, sprinkle in the flour and cook, stirring, for 1-2 minutes. Remove from the heat and beat in the milk a little at a time, then return to the heat and bring to the boil, stirring, until the mixture is very thick and smooth.

2 Remove the pan from the heat and add the chicken, tarragon or parsley, half the lemon zest and salt and pepper to taste. Beat well to mix. Turn the mixture out on to a plate, spread it out evenly and leave until quite cold.

3 Form the mixture into 4 oval croquette shapes. Pour the beaten egg on to a shallow plate, and spread the breadcrumbs mixed with the remaining lemon zest on another plate. Coat the croquettes first in the beaten egg, and then in the breadcrumbs. Press the breadcrumbs on firmly so that they stick to the croquettes. Chill in the refrigerator for at least 30 minutes.

4 Heat the oil in a large frying pan until hot but not smoking. Add the croquettes to the hot oil and fry for 3 minutes on each side, turning once, until the breadcrumbs are golden brown and crisp. Remove with a fish slice and drain on paper towels. Serve hot, with lemon wedges and tarragon or parsley sprigs. A tomato salad and/or a colourful and crunchy mixed salad make ideal accompaniments.

Serves 4
Preparation time: 30 minutes,
plus chilling
Cooking time: 6 minutes

Chicken Liver Risotto

In a genuine Italian risotto, the liquid is added a little at a time, which means that the cook must stand over the pot for the entire cooking time. This recipe cheats a little, but it is much more convenient and less time-consuming – and it works very well.

2 tablespoons extra-virgin olive oil
1 onion, chopped finely
250 g/8 oz chicken livers, cores removed, chopped roughly
1 garlic clove, crushed
300 g/10 oz Italian risotto rice
125 ml/4 fl oz dry white wine
about 1 litre/1¾ pints hot Chicken Stock (see page 8)

large pinch of saffron threads
125 g/4 oz frozen peas or petits pois
salt and pepper

TO FINISH:

6 tablespoons double cream
2 tablespoons chopped fresh flat leaf parsley (optional)
about 50 g/2 oz Parmesan cheese

1 Heat the olive oil in a large flameproof casserole, add the onion and fry over a gentle heat, stirring frequently, for about 5 minutes until softened but not coloured.

2 Add the chicken livers and the crushed garlic, increase the heat to moderate and fry, stirring constantly, for 2-3 minutes, or until the livers change colour on all sides.

3 Add the rice, stir well, then add the wine and stir until the bubbles subside.

4 Pour in 600 ml/1 pint of the hot stock, add the saffron and salt and pepper to taste and stir well. Bring to the boil, then cover and simmer over a gentle heat for 10 minutes, stirring occasionally to prevent the rice sticking to the bottom of the pan.

5 Add a further 400 ml/14 fl oz hot stock to the risotto, stir well to combine, then add the peas. Cover and simmer for a further 10 minutes, stirring occasionally and adding a little more stock if necessary.

6 Remove the pan from the heat and gently fold in the cream and the parsley (if using). Adjust the seasoning to taste. Serve hot, topped with shavings of Parmesan. A crisp green or mixed salad is the only accompaniment needed for this hearty lunch or supper dish.

Serves 4
Preparation time: 15-20 minutes
Cooking time: 20 minutes

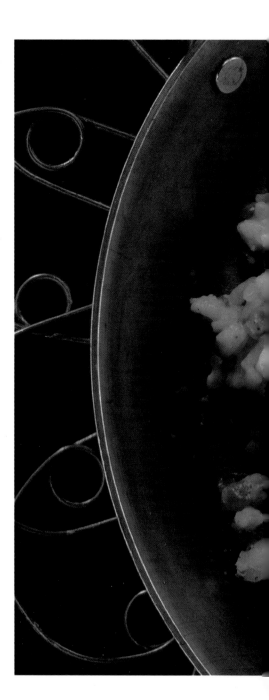

Turkey Tetrazzini

A favourite American dish, made popular by Italian emigrés in the United States. If you make it with leftover Christmas turkey, omit the poaching stage and use turkey or chicken stock as the cooking liquid.

375 g/12 oz turkey breast steaks
1 onion, quartered
1 celery stick, chopped roughly
1 bouquet garni
a few black peppercorns
750 ml/1¼ pints water
4 tablespoons dry sherry
1 tablespoon extra-virgin olive oil
250 g/8 oz spaghetti
40 g/1½ oz butter
40 g/1½ oz plain flour
125 ml/4 fl oz double cream
good pinch of mustard powder
3 tablespoons freshly grated
   Parmesan cheese
salt and pepper
celery leaves, to garnish (optional)

1 Put the turkey steaks in a wide shallow pan with the onion, celery, bouquet garni, peppercorns and a pinch of salt. Pour in the water, add the sherry and bring to the boil over a moderate heat. Lower the heat, cover and poach for 20 minutes or until the turkey is tender when pierced with a skewer or fork.
2 Remove the pan from the heat and leave the turkey to cool in the poaching liquid.

3 Remove the turkey from the liquid, strain the liquid into a measuring jug and make up to 600 ml/1 pint with water if necessary. Cut the turkey into thin strips.
4 Bring a large saucepan of water to the boil, then add ½ teaspoon salt and the oil. Add the spaghetti and boil, uncovered, over a moderate heat for 10 minutes, or according to packet instructions, until *al dente*.
5 Meanwhile, melt the butter in a saucepan, sprinkle in the flour and cook over a moderate heat, stirring, for 1-2 minutes. Gradually pour in the strained poaching liquid, beating vigorously with a balloon whisk or wooden spoon after each addition. Bring to the boil, stirring all the time, then lower the heat and simmer, stirring, for about 5 minutes until thickened and smooth.

6 Remove the pan from the heat and stir in the cream, mustard and salt and pepper to taste. Add the turkey strips and fold gently to mix.
7 Drain the spaghetti and spread half in the bottom of a lightly oiled ovenproof dish. Cover with half the turkey mixture, then the remaining spaghetti. Top with remaining turkey and sprinkle with the Parmesan.
8 Place in a preheated oven, 200°C (400°F), Gas Mark 6 for 10 minutes or until golden. Serve hot, garnished with celery leaves and accompanied by a green salad.

Serves 4
Preparation time: 30 minutes,
plus cooling
Cooking time: 10 minutes
Oven temperature: 200°C (400°F),
Gas Mark 6

Club Sandwich

This famous American sandwich always has three layers of white bread, but you can use granary or wholemeal if you like. Turkey is traditional, but chicken makes a good substitute.

6 rindless streaky bacon rashers
6 slices of white bread
6 tablespoons mayonnaise
8 small lettuce leaves
2 large slices of cooked turkey
2 tomatoes, sliced thinly
salt and pepper

1 Cook the bacon in a heavy-based frying pan or under a preheated hot grill for 5-7 minutes, turning once, until crisp on both sides. Remove and drain on paper towels.
2 Toast the bread on both sides, then cut off and discard the crusts.
3 Arrange the toasted bread slices on a large board or work surface and spread one side of each slice with mayonnaise.
4 Arrange 2 of the lettuce leaves on each of 2 slices of toast and sprinkle with salt and pepper to taste.
5 Arrange 1 slice of turkey on top of the lettuce on each sandwich, then top with another slice of toast, with the mayonnaise-side up. Arrange the remaining lettuce leaves on top and add the tomato slices, then the crisp bacon, cutting the rashers to fit wherever necessary.

6 Cover with the remaining 2 slices of bread, mayonnaise side down. Leave the sandwiches whole, or cut into 4 triangles and pierce with long cocktail sticks. Serve immediately.

Ice-cold beer is the traditional accompaniment.

Serves 2
Preparation time: about 20 minutes

Old English Chicken and Vegetable Pie

The Elizabethans used spices with meat and poultry, far more than we do today. More chicken stock can be substituted for the cider.

2 tablespoons rapeseed oil
12 skinned and boned chicken thighs,
    cut into small bite-sized pieces
15 g/½ oz butter
375 g/12 oz carrots, sliced thickly
375 g/12 oz turnips or parsnips,
    sliced thickly
2 leeks, trimmed, cleaned and
    sliced thickly

2 tablespoons plain flour
½ teaspoon ground mixed spice
300 ml/½ pint dry cider
150 ml/¼ pint Chicken Stock
    (see page 8)
250 g/8 oz puff pastry, thawed
    if frozen
beaten egg, to glaze
salt and pepper

1 Heat the oil in a flameproof casserole. Sauté the chicken over a moderate heat for about 5 minutes until coloured on all sides. Remove and set aside on a plate.
2 Melt the butter in the casserole, then add the vegetables and toss to coat in the oil and butter. Lower the heat, cover and sweat gently for 10 minutes.
3 Sprinkle in the flour and mixed spice. Cook, stirring, for 1-2 minutes, then gradually stir in the cider and stock. Bring to the boil, stirring, season to taste, and add the chicken with any juices from the plate. Cover and cook over a gentle heat for 10 minutes. Turn into a bowl and leave until cold.
4 Roll out the pastry on a lightly floured surface and cut out a lid to fit a 1 litre/2 pint pie dish. Cut out a strip of pastry to go around the rim of the dish. From the trimmings, cut out pastry leaves for the top of the pie.
5 Spoon the cold mixture into the pie dish, putting a pie funnel in the centre. Brush the rim of the dish with water. Press the pastry strip into place, brush with water, and put the lid on top, cutting a hole for the pie funnel.
6 Press the edges to seal, knock up and flute. Brush the pastry with beaten egg and stick the pastry leaves on top. Brush again with beaten egg.
7 Place in a preheated oven, 220°C (425°F), Gas Mark 7 for 30 minutes or until the pastry is crisp and golden. Serve hot, straight from the dish, with a fresh green vegetable and creamed or mashed potatoes.

Serves 4
Preparation time: 45 minutes, plus cooling
Cooking time: 30 minutes
Oven temperature: 220°C (425°F), Gas Mark 7

VARIATION

Chicken Pot Pie

1 Boil 750 g/1½ lb old potatoes until just tender. Drain and slice into thin rounds.
2 Make a white sauce with 50 g/2 oz butter, 40 g/1½ oz plain flour and 600 ml/1 pint milk. Add 2 tablespoons finely chopped fresh parsley and ¼ teaspoon mustard powder. Stir in about 375 g/12 oz skinned and boned cooked chicken, cut into pieces, and 200 g/7 oz frozen mixed vegetables, thawed. Add salt and pepper to taste.
3 Pour the mixture into a pie dish, arrange 3 hard-boiled eggs, shelled and sliced, on top, then add the potato rounds. Brush with melted butter and sprinkle with 50 g/2 oz grated cheese (such as Double Gloucester or Red Leicester). Cook in a preheated oven, 190°C (375°F), Gas Mark 5 for 30 minutes until the potatoes are crisp and golden.

Serves 4
Preparation time: about 30 minutes
Cooking time: 30 minutes
Oven temperature: 190°C (375°F), Gas Mark 5

Christmas Turkey and Vegetable Soup

This is a soup with endless possibilities – try adding 1-2 teaspoons curry powder or garam masala when frying the onion at the beginning. Turkey goes very well with curry, and so too do parsnips, green peas and cheese.

2 tablespoons rapeseed oil
1 onion, chopped finely
2-3 celery sticks, sliced thickly
3 carrots, sliced thickly
3 parsnips, chopped
1.2 litres/2 pints Turkey Stock (see
   page 9), or chicken, vegetable, or
   other light stock
1 teaspoon tomato purée
125 g/4 oz small pasta shapes
125 g/4 oz frozen peas
250-375 g/8-12 oz skinned and
   boned cooked turkey, cut into
   bite-sized pieces
salt and pepper
grated Cheddar or other hard cheese,
   to serve

1 Heat the oil in a large saucepan, add the onion and fry gently, stirring frequently, for about 5 minutes until softened but not coloured.
2 Add the celery, carrots and parsnips and stir to mix, then cook, stirring, for a further 5 minutes.

3 Add the stock, tomato purée and salt and pepper and stir well. Bring to the boil over a high heat, stirring, then lower the heat to moderate. Cover the pan and simmer, stirring occasionally, for about 15 minutes.
4 Add the pasta and peas. Cook for 10 minutes or until the pasta is *al dente*. Add the turkey and heat through for another 5 minutes. Taste for seasoning. Serve hot in warmed bowls, sprinkled with grated cheese.

Serves 4-6
Preparation time: 10-15 minutes
Cooking time: about 40 minutes

Chow Mein

2 tablespoons rapeseed oil
4 spring onions or 1 onion,
    sliced thinly
2.5 cm/1 inch piece of fresh root
    ginger, crushed
1 garlic clove, crushed
250 g/8 oz skinned chicken breast
    fillets, cut diagonally into thin strips
1 x 250 g/8 oz packet Chinese
    egg noodles
125 g/4 oz mangetout, topped and
    tailed, cut crossways if large
125 g/4 oz boiled ham, cut into
    thin strips
2-3 tablespoons soy sauce, to taste
2 tablespoons rice wine or dry sherry
2 teaspoons sesame oil
1 teaspoon sugar
salt and pepper

1 Heat a wok or large deep frying pan over a moderate heat until hot. Add the oil and heat until hot but not smoking. Add the spring onions or onion, ginger and garlic and stir-fry over a gentle heat for 1-2 minutes until softened but not coloured.

2 Add the strips of chicken breast and stir-fry over a moderate heat for 3-4 minutes until they change colour on all sides.

3 Meanwhile, put the egg noodles in a large bowl and cover with boiling water. Leave to stand.

4 Add the mangetout to the chicken in the wok and stir-fry for 2-3 minutes until the chicken is tender when pierced with a skewer or fork.

5 Drain the noodles, add to the wok with the ham, and toss over a high heat until hot. Add the soy sauce, rice wine or sherry, sesame oil, sugar and season to taste. Toss until all the ingredients are hot and glistening. Serve immediately.

Serves 3-4
Preparation time: 20 minutes
Cooking time: about 10 minutes

Chicken in a Brick

This is a healthy way to cook – no added fat is required and the chicken is moist and tender because it loses none of its natural juices. To make a rich and creamy sauce for a special occasion, add a few tablespoons of crème fraîche to the vegetables before serving.

1 x 2 kg/4 lb oven-ready chicken,
   giblets removed
2 onions, quartered
2 garlic cloves, quartered
4 small young carrots, cut
   into strips

1 teaspoon dried tarragon
2 teaspoons chopped fresh tarragon
salt and pepper

1 Soak the chicken brick in cold water for 30 minutes.
2 Wash the inside of the chicken and dry with paper towels. Put half the onion and garlic into the cavity with salt and pepper to taste.
3 Remove the chicken brick from the water and put the bird in the bottom half, surrounded with the carrots and the remaining onion and garlic quarters. Sprinkle with the dried tarragon and season to taste. Cover with the top half of the brick and place in a cold oven. Set the oven to 230°C (450°F), Gas Mark 8 and cook for exactly 2 hours without opening the oven door.
4 Lift the chicken out of the brick and remove and discard the onion and garlic from the cavity. Drain off most of the cooking juices from the vegetables in the brick, then stir the fresh tarragon into the vegetables. Serve the chicken on a warmed serving platter, surrounded by the cooked vegetables. New potatoes, boiled or steamed, and a fresh seasonal green vegetable would make good accompaniments.

Serves 4
Preparation time: 10 minutes
Cooking time: 2 hours
Oven temperature: 230°C (450°F), Gas Mark 8

Turkey in a Brick with Cranberries and Orange

1 Prepare the chicken brick as in the main recipe, then put 250 g/8 oz fresh or thawed frozen cranberries in the bottom half. Add the grated zest and juice of 1 orange and 2 tablespoons soft brown sugar. Stir well. Lay sprigs of thyme on top.
2 Soften 50 g/2 oz butter and beat in the grated zest of 1 orange with salt and pepper to taste. Lift the skin away from a bone-in turkey breast of about 2 kg/4 lb, and spread the softened butter all over the flesh. Press the skin back into place.
3 Put the turkey, skin-side up, on the bed of cranberries. Season to taste. Cover with the top half of the brick and place in a cold oven. Set the oven to 230°C (450°F), Gas Mark 8 and cook for exactly 2 hours without opening the oven door.
4 Lift the turkey out of the brick and place on a warmed serving platter. Remove the cranberries with a slotted spoon and arrange around the turkey. Garnish with fresh thyme and serve the juices separately.

Serves 4
Preparation time: 10 minutes
Cooking time: 2 hours
Oven temperature: 230°C (450°F), Gas Mark 8

Coronation Chicken

To make this favourite classic English recipe, buy a roasted chicken, or you can poach the chicken yourself, as in the recipe for Chicken and Grape Salad (page 23).

1 x 1.5 kg/3 lb cold cooked chicken
1 tablespoon rapeseed oil
1 onion, chopped finely
1 tablespoon curry paste
1 tablespoon tomato purée
2 tablespoons lemon juice
125 g/4 oz dried apricot halves,
    soaked in dry white wine to cover
    for 20-30 minutes
125 ml/4 fl oz double or whipping
    cream
300 ml/½ pint mayonnaise
salt and pepper
chervil, to garnish (optional)

1 Remove the chicken meat from the bones and cut it into bite-sized pieces, discarding the skin. Set the chicken aside.
2 Heat the oil in a small saucepan, add the onion and fry gently, stirring frequently, for about 5 minutes until softened but not coloured.
3 Add the curry paste, tomato purée and lemon juice and stir well to mix, then cook for 5 minutes, stirring frequently. Remove from the heat and work through a small sieve. Set the mixture aside.

4 Drain the apricots and reserve the soaking liquid. Work the apricots to a purée in a food processor or blender, with a little of the soaking liquid if necessary. Mix the purée with the curried onion.
5 Whip the cream until it is just thick. Stir the curried apricot mixture into the mayonnaise, then carefully fold in the whipped cream. Add salt and pepper to taste.
6 Fold the chicken into the curried apricot mayonnaise until evenly

coated. Cover and chill in the refrigerator for at least 2 hours to allow the flavours to mingle.
7 Before serving, uncover the salad and allow to come to room temperature for 30 minutes to 1 hour. Adjust the seasoning to taste, garnish with chervil if liked, and serve with a rice or pasta salad.

Serves 6
Preparation time: 30 minutes, plus soaking and chilling

Poulet Bonne Femme

A classic French dish which is even better if the chicken is sprinkled with a little wine just before putting it in the oven.

1 x 2 kg/4 lb oven-ready chicken, giblets removed
1 onion, quartered
16 small pickling onions
500 g/1 lb small new potatoes
125 g/4 oz streaky bacon rashers, rinds removed, chopped
25 g/1 oz butter
1 tablespoon extra-virgin olive oil
1 bouquet garni
salt and pepper
a bunch of herbs, to garnish

1 Wash the chicken cavity and dry with paper towels. Insert the onion and season to taste. Truss the chicken with string and set aside.
2 In a saucepan, cover the pickling onions with cold water. Bring to the boil over a moderate heat, cover and simmer for 5 minutes. Drain and plunge into cold water. Peel off the skins. Repeat the same process for the potatoes.
3 Fry the bacon gently in a large flameproof casserole, stirring frequently, for about 5 minutes until the fat runs. Fry over a moderate heat for a further 5 minutes or until the bacon begins to crisp. Remove and drain on paper towels.

4 Heat the butter and oil in the casserole until sizzling and sauté the chicken until golden on all sides.
5 Put the potatoes and onions around the chicken, sprinkle it with bacon and tuck in the bouquet garni.
6 Season with a little salt and plenty of black pepper, cover and place in a preheated oven, 170°C (325°F), Gas Mark 3 for 2¼-2½ hours until the juices run clear. Baste several times during roasting.
7 Lift the bird out of the casserole, cover tightly with foil and set aside to rest in a warm place for about 10 minutes. Discard the bouquet garni, and keep the vegetables hot.
8 Discard the trussing string and put the chicken on a warmed serving platter, surrounded with the vegetables and garnished with herbs. Serve with a green vegetable.

Serves 4
Preparation time: 20 minutes
Cooking time: 2¼-2½ hours
Oven temperature: 170°C (325°F), Gas Mark 3

Chicken and Sweetcorn Chowder

Rich and creamy, this American-style soup is substantial enough to serve as a main dish with crusty bread. The cream added at the end is not essential if you prefer a dish that is less rich. Take care when adding salt as the bacon may be salty, especially if it is smoked.

1 tablespoon rapeseed oil

125 g /4 oz streaky bacon rashers, rinds removed, chopped

1 large onion, chopped finely

500 g/1 lb potatoes, diced

½ teaspoon dried mixed herbs

600 ml/1 pint milk

450 ml/¾ pint water

1 bay leaf

250-375 g/8-12 oz skinned and boned cooked chicken, diced

1 x 325 g/11 oz can sweetcorn and peppers, drained

150 ml/¼ pint single cream (optional)

salt and pepper

finely chopped fresh parsley, to garnish

1 Heat the oil in a large saucepan or flameproof casserole, add the bacon and fry over a moderate heat for about 5 minutes until crispy. Remove the bacon with a slotted spoon and drain on paper towels. Chop or crumble the crispy bacon into pieces.

2 Add the onion to the pan and fry over a gentle heat, stirring frequently, for about 5 minutes until softened but not coloured. Add the diced potatoes and mixed herbs and stir to mix with the onion, then add the milk, water, bay leaf, and salt and pepper to taste.

3 Bring to the boil over a high heat, stirring, then lower the heat to moderate. Cover and simmer, stirring occasionally, for 20 minutes or until the potatoes are tender when pierced with a skewer or fork. Discard the bay leaf.

4 Add the chicken and sweetcorn and peppers. Heat through for about 5 minutes, then lower the heat and stir in the cream, if using. Adjust the seasoning to taste. Serve hot, sprinkled with the chopped crispy bacon and chopped parsley.

Serves 4
Preparation time: 20 minutes
Cooking time: about 30 minutes

VARIATION

Turkey and Chestnut Soup

Another delicious soup recipe, and an excellent way to use up leftover Christmas turkey.

1 Break the turkey carcass into pieces and place in a large saucepan with any leftover stuffing, 1 onion, 1 carrot and 1 celery stick, all chopped, 2 sprigs of thyme and salt and pepper. Add 1.8 litres/ 3 pints water and bring to the boil. Cover and simmer for 3 hours. Add extra water when necessary.

2 Remove the carcass and vegetables and discard. Strain the stock and add any reserved turkey meat cut into bite-sized pieces. Heat 2 tablespoons oil in the rinsed-out pan. Add 2 large potatoes, 1 onion, 1 carrot and 1 celery stick, all chopped. Cook gently, stirring, for 5 minutes, pour in the strained stock and bring to the boil. Simmer for about 20 minutes and add 475 g/15 oz canned whole chestnuts in brine, drained, and 3 tablespoons sherry or port. Reheat, check seasoning and serve hot, garnished with thyme.

Serves 6
Preparation time: 20 minutes
Cooking time: 3½ hours

Chicken Marengo

A French classic, created for Napoleon after the Battle of Marengo.

1 onion, chopped finely

1 garlic clove, crushed

3 tablespoons rapeseed oil

8 skinned and boned chicken thighs, cut into bite-sized pieces

50 ml/2 fl oz Cognac

250 g/8 oz button mushrooms, sliced thinly

1 x 250 g/8 oz can peeled plum tomatoes

250 ml/8 fl oz dry white wine

2 rosemary sprigs

1 teaspoon dried mixed herbs

salt and pepper

TO FINISH:

250 g/8 oz peeled cooked prawns

1-2 tablespoons chopped fresh coriander

1 Fry the onion and garlic in the oil for 5 minutes until softened. Add the chicken and sauté for about 5 minutes until it changes colour on all sides.

2 Gently warm the Cognac in a small saucepan, pour over the chicken and set it alight with a match. When the flames subside, add the sliced button mushrooms and sauté for about 5 minutes. Add the tomatoes, white wine, rosemary, mixed herbs and salt and pepper.

3 Bring to the boil, stirring, then lower the heat, cover and simmer, stirring frequently, for 30 minutes or until the chicken is tender.

4 Discard the rosemary, then add the prawns and coriander. Heat through, taste for seasoning and serve with buttered noodles and a green salad.

Serves 4

Preparation time: 15 minutes

Cooking time: about 50 minutes

Italian Pot-roast Turkey with Risotto Stuffing

1 onion, chopped finely
2 tablespoons extra-virgin olive oil
125 g/4 oz risotto rice
900 ml/1½ pints hot Chicken Stock
   (see pages 8-9)
125 g/4 oz chopped, rindless pancetta
   or smoked streaky bacon rashers
1 medium fennel bulb, chopped
   finely, with feathery tops reserved
2 garlic cloves, chopped finely
50 g/2 oz Parmesan cheese,
   freshly grated
1 egg, beaten
1 x 3 kg/6 lb oven-ready turkey,
   giblets removed
15 g/½ oz butter
4 tablespoons anise-flavoured liqueur
150 ml/¼ pint dry white wine
salt and pepper

1 Gently fry the onion in half the oil in a saucepan, stirring, until softened but not coloured.
2 Stir in the rice, add half the stock and bring to the boil. Stir until the stock is absorbed, then add the remaining stock and return to the boil. Cover and simmer, stirring frequently, for 15 minutes until all the stock is absorbed. Set aside.
3 Gently fry the pancetta or bacon in another pan until the fat starts to run. Add the fennel, garlic and pepper to taste and cook, stirring frequently, for 10 minutes until soft. Add to the rice with half the Parmesan and egg. Stir, check seasoning and leave to cool.
4 Wash and dry the turkey cavity and sprinkle with salt and pepper. Fill the neck end with stuffing and truss with string. Place leftover stuffing in an oiled baking dish and sprinkle with the remaining Parmesan.
5 Heat the remaining oil and butter in a flameproof casserole into which the turkey will just fit. Add the turkey and cook for about 10 minutes, until lightly coloured on all sides.
6 Pour the liqueur over the turkey, allow to sizzle, then pour over the wine and season to taste.
7 Cover and cook in a preheated oven, 180°C (350°F), Gas Mark 4 for 2½-3 hours until tender and the juices run clear when the thickest part of a thigh is pierced with a skewer or fork. Baste occasionally. Place the dish of stuffing in the oven for the last 15-20 minutes, until heated through.
8 Remove the bird, cover tightly with foil and set aside to rest in a warm place for about 15 minutes. Discard the trussing string. Keep the cooking juices hot.
9 Serve the turkey garnished with the reserved fennel tops, with the cooking juices and any stuffing handed separately. Julienne of carrots in a cream sauce or the Italian vegetable dish of spinach tossed with pine nuts and raisins would be excellent accompaniments.

Serves 6-8
Preparation time: 50 minutes
Cooking time: 2½-3 hours
Oven temperature: 180°C (350°F), Gas Mark 4

Pollo Tonnato

Traditionally made with veal and called Vitello Tonnato in Italian, this chicken dish is lighter than the veal, but equally good. Another delicious variation is Tacchino Tonnato, made with turkey breast.

300 ml/½ pint Chicken Stock (see page 8)
150 ml/¼ pint dry white wine
1 onion, sliced thickly
1 celery stick, sliced thickly
1 small bunch of fresh tarragon
6 black peppercorns
8 large skinned chicken breast fillets
1 x 200 g/7 oz can tuna in oil, drained
1 x 50 g/2 oz can anchovy fillets in oil, drained
2 egg yolks
2 tablespoons lemon juice, more to taste
150 ml/¼ pint extra-virgin olive oil
TO GARNISH:
capers
sprigs of flat leaf parsley
nasturtium flowers and leaves (optional)

1 Put the chicken stock, wine, onion, celery, tarragon, peppercorns and ½ teaspoon salt in a wide shallow pan. Bring to the boil over a moderate heat, then lower the heat to a gentle simmer.
2 Add the chicken breasts, cover the pan and poach gently for 20 minutes or until tender when pierced with a skewer or fork.

3 Remove the chicken from the stock and set aside to cool on paper towels. Strain the liquid through a sieve, return to the pan and boil rapidly until reduced to about 75 ml/3 fl oz. Pour into a jug and set aside to cool.
4 Put the tuna and anchovies in a food processor or blender and work to a smooth purée. Add the egg yolks and the lemon juice and work again. Gradually add the olive oil in a thin, steady stream as for making mayonnaise, then add enough of the reduced cooking liquid to give a thin coating consistency. Work again to make as smooth a purée as possible.

5 Arrange the chicken breasts on a serving platter and spoon over the sauce to coat them completely. Cover loosely with foil (which should not touch the sauce) and chill in the refrigerator overnight.
6 Before serving, uncover the chicken and allow to come to room temperature for 30-60 minutes. Garnish with capers, parsley and nasturtiums. Serve with mixed rice and a green salad.

Serves 8
Preparation time: 1 hour, plus cooling and chilling
Cooking time: 20 minutes

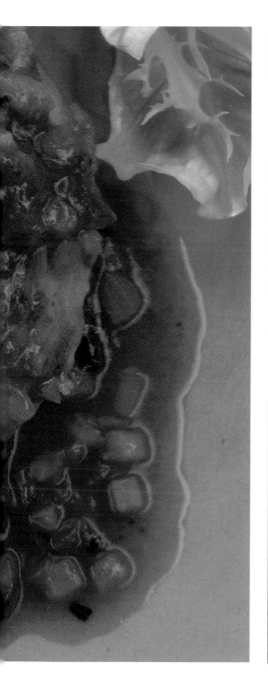

Pollo alla Cacciatora

Porcini – Italian dried mushrooms – are available at most delicatessens and some good supermarkets. Though expensive, they are full of flavour, so you need only a very small quantity.

15 g/½ oz dried mushrooms
150 ml/¼ pint warm water
2 tablespoons extra-virgin olive oil
4 skinned chicken portions
1 onion, chopped finely
1 large carrot, chopped finely
1 large celery stick, chopped finely
2 garlic cloves, crushed
150 ml/¼ pint Italian dry white wine

1 x 400 g/14 oz can peeled
   plum tomatoes
1 tablespoon tomato purée
1 teaspoon dried oregano
1 teaspoon dried mixed herbs
large pinch of sugar
salt and pepper
chopped fresh flat leaf parsley,
   to garnish

1 Soak the dried mushrooms in the warm water in a bowl for 20 minutes.
2 Meanwhile, heat the oil in a large flameproof casserole, add the chicken and sauté over a moderate heat for 7-10 minutes until golden on all sides. Remove with a slotted spoon and set aside on a plate.
3 Add the onion, carrot, celery and garlic to the casserole and fry over a gentle heat, stirring frequently, for 7-10 minutes until softened.
4 Drain the mushrooms and reserve the soaking liquid. Chop or slice the mushrooms finely.
5 Add the mushrooms to the casserole with the reserved soaking liquid and the wine, increase the heat to moderate and stir until bubbling. Add the tomatoes with their juice, stir well with a wooden spoon to break them up, then add the tomato purée, herbs, sugar and salt and pepper to taste.
6 Return the chicken to the casserole with the juices that have collected on the plate. Cover and simmer over a gentle heat, stirring occasionally, for 40 minutes or until the chicken is tender when pierced with a skewer or fork. Adjust the seasoning to taste. Serve hot, sprinkled with chopped fresh parsley. Hot Italian ciabatta bread, together with a rocket or mixed leaf salad, would be the perfect accompaniments.

Serves 4
Preparation time: 20 minutes
Cooking time: about 50 minutes

Pollo alla Valdostana

Fontina is a mountain cheese from the Val d'Aosta in Northern Italy.

6 skinned, part-boned chicken breasts
½ teaspoon dried oregano
½ teaspoon dried basil
2 tablespoons extra-virgin olive oil
3 thin slices of Parma ham
    (prosciutto di Parma), total weight
    about 75 g/3 oz
2 garlic cloves, crushed
2 tablespoons balsamic vinegar
6 tablespoons dry Italian vermouth or
    white wine
3 thin slices of Fontina cheese, total
    weight about 75 g/3 oz
salt and pepper
basil sprigs, to garnish

1 Sprinkle the slit in each chicken breast with the dried herbs and add salt and pepper to taste.
2 Heat the oil in a large sauté pan. Add the chicken breasts and sauté over a moderate heat for 1-2 minutes on each side until they just change colour. Remove with a slotted spoon until cool enough to handle. Reserve the oil.
3 Cut the slices of Parma ham in half. Stuff each chicken breast with a piece of ham, then place the breasts in a single layer in a lightly oiled ovenproof dish.

4 Return the pan to the heat, add the garlic and balsamic vinegar and stir until sizzling. Stir in the vermouth or wine. Pour over the chicken breasts.
5 Halve each slice of Fontina cheese, and put a slice on top of each chicken breast.
6 Place in a preheated oven, 200°C (400°F), Gas Mark 6 for 20 minutes or until the Fontina melts and the chicken is tender. Add pepper and

serve hot, with sauté potatoes and green beans or a green salad. Garnish with basil.

Serves 6
Preparation time: 15 minutes
Cooking time: about 25 minutes
Oven temperature: 200°C (400°F), Gas Mark 6

Spanish Paella

1 kg/2 lb fresh mussels
4 garlic cloves
1 bunch of fresh mixed herbs
150 ml/¼ pint dry white wine
about 2 litres/3½ pints Chicken Stock
    (see page 8) or water
4 small squid, cleaned and sliced
    into rings
4 tablespoons extra-virgin olive oil
1 large onion, chopped finely
1 red pepper, cored, deseeded and
    chopped
4 large ripe tomatoes, skinned,
    deseeded and chopped
12 skinned and boned chicken thighs,
    cut into bite-sized pieces
500 g/1 lb short-grain rice
125 g/4 oz fresh or frozen peas
12 large raw prawns, peeled (optional)
salt and pepper
chopped parsley, to garnish

1 Scrub the mussels with a small stiff brush, scraping off the beards and and barnacles with a small sharp knife. Discard any open mussels.
2 Slice 2 garlic cloves and crush the remainder. Put the slices in a large saucepan with the herbs, wine, 150 ml/¼ pint stock or water and season to taste. Add the mussels, cover the pan tightly and bring to the boil. Shake the pan vigorously and simmer for about 5 minutes until the mussels open. Remove the mussels from the liquid and set aside, discarding any which remain closed. Strain the liquid and reserve.

3 Sauté the squid in half the oil for 5 minutes, stirring frequently.
4 Add the onion, red pepper and crushed garlic and cook gently, stirring frequently, for 5 minutes until softened. Add the mussel cooking liquid, tomatoes and seasoning. Bring to the boil, stirring, then simmer gently, stirring, for 15-20 minutes until the mixture is concentrated and thick. Transfer to a bowl.
5 Sauté the chicken in the remaining oil for 5 minutes. Add the rice and turn it in the oil for a few minutes. Stir the squid mixture into the pan. Add about one third of the remaining stock and bring to the boil, stirring.
6 Boil rapidly for 3-4 minutes, cover and simmer for 30 minutes. Add

more stock as the rice becomes dry and stir frequently, moving the rice into the centre so it cooks evenly. The paella is ready when the chicken is tender, the rice is *al dente* and almost all the liquid absorbed.
7 Check seasoning, add the peas and prawns and simmer, stirring, for 5 minutes or until they are cooked, adding stock or water if required.
8 Arrange the mussels decoratively on top of the paella, cover tightly with foil and cook for 5 minutes or until the mussels are hot. Sprinkle with the parsley if liked, and serve.

Serves 6
Preparation time: about 40 minutes
Cooking time: about 1¼ hours

Coq au Vin

A great French classic, well worth reviving for its rich and heady flavour. In an interesting modern variation, the traditional red wine is replaced with a dry white such as Chablis, and the dish is garnished with fried croûtes, the edges dipped in finely chopped parsley.

1 x 2 kg/4 lb oven-ready chicken,
   giblets removed, cut into
   8 pieces
2 teaspoons dried thyme
3 tablespoons rapeseed oil
175 g/6 oz rindless smoked streaky
   bacon rashers, chopped
16 small pickling onions, blanched
   and peeled
250 g/8 oz small button mushrooms

3 garlic cloves, crushed
3 tablespoons Cognac
350 ml/12 fl oz red wine
1 bouquet garni
1 tablespoon butter
2 tablespoons plain flour
salt and pepper
TO GARNISH:
fresh thyme (optional)
fresh parsley (optional)

1 Rub the chicken with the dried thyme and pepper. Sauté half the pieces in the oil in a large flameproof casserole for 7-10 minutes until golden. Remove with a slotted spoon and set aside on a plate. Repeat with the remaining chicken.

2 Add the bacon to the casserole and cook over a moderate heat, stirring frequently, until the fat runs. Add the onions, mushrooms and garlic and cook, stirring frequently, for 5 minutes.

3 Gently warm the Cognac in a small saucepan. Return the chicken and its juices to the casserole, pour in the Cognac and set it alight with a match. When the flames subside, add the wine, and bring to the boil, stirring. Add the bouquet garni, salt and pepper to taste. Cover and simmer over a gentle heat, stirring occasionally, for 40 minutes or until the chicken is tender.

4 Remove the chicken and vegetables with a slotted spoon and keep hot. Discard the bouquet garni. Mix the butter and flour to a paste and add to the sauce a little at a time until evenly blended. Bring to the boil and simmer, stirring, for 2-3 minutes until the sauce thickens. Adjust the seasoning to taste.

5 Serve the chicken and vegetables with the sauce spooned over, and garnished with thyme and parsley if liked.

Serves 4
Preparation time: 30 minutes
Cooking time: about 50 minutes

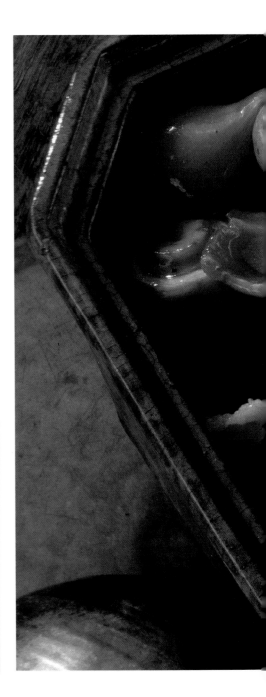

Chicken Couscous

This North African stew is the ultimate one-pot dish.

125 g/4 oz chick peas, soaked in cold
   water overnight, then drained
2 onions, chopped finely
3 garlic cloves, chopped finely
2 teaspoons ground coriander
2 teaspoons cumin
2 teaspoons turmeric
2 teaspoons chilli powder
2 tablespoons extra-virgin olive oil
2 tablespoons tomato purée
12 skinned and boned chicken thighs,
   cut into large bite-sized pieces

500 g/1 lb couscous
½ teaspoon ground cinnamon
few drops of orange flower water
4 carrots, sliced thickly
2 parsnips, sliced thickly
2 potatoes, cut into chunks
50 g/2 oz butter
4 courgettes, sliced thickly
2 tablespoons sultanas or raisins
harissa sauce, to taste
salt and pepper
fresh coriander, to garnish

1 Simmer the chick peas for 1 hour in a large saucepan, half-covered.
2 Gently fry the onions, garlic and ground spices in the oil in the bottom of a couscousière or large saucepan, for about 5 minutes until softened.
3 Stir in tomato purée, drained chick peas and seasoning. Cover with water and bring to the boil, stirring. Simmer, stirring occasionally, for 1 hour. Top up with water to keep the chick peas covered. Add the chicken and simmer, covered, for about 20 minutes. Stir occasionally.
4 Meanwhile, put the couscous in a bowl and cover with boiling water. Add the cinnamon and orange flower water and stir.
5 Add the carrots, parsnips and potatoes to the chicken mixture, stir, cover with water and bring to the boil again.
6 Put the couscous and half the butter in the steamer on top of the couscousière (or in a fine-meshed sieve over the saucepan). Cover and cook for 30 minutes or until the chicken and vegetables are tender, adding the courgettes and sultanas or raisins halfway through.
7 Remove the couscous, check the chicken for seasoning, add the harissa sauce to taste and stir well.
8 Fork the remaining butter into the couscous and arrange the couscous in a ring on a dish with the chicken and vegetables in the centre. Garnish with coriander and serve extra harissa sauce separately.

Serves 6-8
Preparation time: 40 minutes,
plus soaking
Cooking time: about 2¾ hours

Moroccan Tagine

2 teaspoons turmeric
2 teaspoons paprika
1 teaspoon ground cinnamon
12 skinned and boned chicken thighs,
  cut into bite-sized pieces
2 tablespoons extra-virgin olive oil
1 onion, chopped finely
2.5 cm/1 inch piece of fresh root
  ginger, crushed
1 garlic clove, crushed
600 ml/1 pint Chicken Stock (page 8)
250 g/8 oz mixed dried fruit (prunes,
  apricots, apples, pears, peaches)
salt and pepper

1 Mix all the spices, season to taste, then use to coat the chicken.

2 Heat the oil in a flameproof casserole, and cook the chicken over a moderate heat, stirring constantly, for 5 minutes until it changes colour on all sides. Remove the pieces with a slotted spoon and set aside on a plate to collect the juices.

3 Add the onion, ginger and garlic to the casserole and cook over a gentle heat, stirring frequently, for about 5 minutes until softened.

4 Gradually stir in the chicken stock, increase the heat to high and bring to the boil. Add the mixed dried fruit and return the chicken and its juices to the casserole. Stir well to mix.

5 Cover and simmer gently, stirring occasionally, for 40 minutes until the chicken is tender when pierced with a skewer or fork. Adjust the seasoning to taste. Serve hot, with plain boiled rice.

Serves 4
Preparation time: 15 minutes
Cooking time: about 50 minutes

Persian Chicken

Sweet and sticky perfumed sauces are popular in Persian cookery, especially with chicken. This one is fruity and spicy, a combination that counterbalances the sweetness beautifully.

2 tablespoons rapeseed oil
25 g/1 oz butter
1 small onion, chopped finely
½ teaspoon ground cinnamon
½ teaspoon turmeric
½ teaspoon paprika
4 cardamom pods, bruised
8 chicken drumsticks, skinned

thinly pared zest of 1 large orange
300 ml/½ pint Chicken Stock (see
   page 8)
6 tablespoons orange juice
2 tablespoons lemon juice
1 teaspoon soft brown sugar
salt and pepper
toasted flaked almonds, to garnish

1 Heat the oil and butter in a large sauté or frying pan. Add the onion and spices and fry over a gentle heat, stirring frequently, for about 5 minutes until the onion is softened but not browned.
2 Add the drumsticks and stir to coat in the spiced onion mixture. Increase the heat to moderate and fry, turning constantly, for 7-10 minutes until the chicken changes colour on all sides.
3 Add the orange zest, stock, orange and lemon juices, sugar and salt and pepper to taste. Bring to the boil, stirring and spooning the sauce over the chicken. Lower the heat, cover and simmer gently for about 30 minutes until the drumsticks are tender when pierced with a skewer or fork. Shake the pan frequently during this time and turn the drumsticks over to ensure they cook evenly.
4 Remove the drumsticks from the cooking liquid, cover and keep warm. Boil the cooking liquid, if necessary, until reduced to a syrupy consistency, then remove and discard the orange zest and taste the sauce for seasoning. Serve the drumsticks fanned out on a bed of rice, coated with sauce and sprinkled with toasted flaked almonds.

Serves 4
Preparation time: 10-15 minutes
Cooking time: about 40 minutes

VARIATION

St Clement's Chicken

An English recipe using oranges and lemons – named after London's famous bells. You can use other fruit juices instead, such as orange and apricot, or tropical fruit.

1 Sauté 6 part-boned chicken breasts in 2 tablespoons rapeseed oil and 15 g/½ oz butter for about 10 minutes until golden. Remove with a slotted spoon and set aside on a plate.
2 Sprinkle in 1 tablespoon plain flour and cook, stirring, for 1-2 minutes. Gradually blend in 250 ml/8 fl oz unsweetened orange juice, stirring, then add 250 ml/8 fl oz chicken stock and the finely grated zest and juice of 3 lemon. Bring to the boil, stirring, then lower the heat and add 2 teaspoons finely chopped fresh sage, and salt and pepper to taste.
3 Return the chicken and its juices to the pan, cover and simmer for 20 minutes until tender. Turn and baste during this time. Check seasoning.
4 Garnish with orange and lemon twists and sage, and serve with buttered noodles and a green salad.

Serves 6
Preparation time: 5-10 minutes
Cooking time: about 30 minutes

Circassian Chicken

*From North Africa to India,
nuts are used as a thickener for
sauces. Walnuts are traditional
in this Middle Eastern dish, but
you can use almonds, hazelnuts
or a mixture of nuts.*

1 x 2 kg/4 lb oven-ready chicken,
  giblets removed
2 celery sticks, chopped roughly
1 large onion, quartered lengthways
2 carrots, chopped roughly
1 large bouquet garni
8 black peppercorns
1.5-1.8 litres/2½-3 pints water
125 g/4 oz shelled walnuts
large pinch of ground cinnamon
large pinch of ground cloves
salt and pepper
TO GARNISH:
2 tablespoons extra-virgin olive oil
1 teaspoon paprika
sprigs of fresh coriander or
  1 tablespoon chopped (optional)

1 Put the chicken in a large
saucepan or flameproof casserole,
add the celery, onion, carrots,
bouquet garni, peppercorns and
1 teaspoon salt. Add enough of the
water to cover and bring to the boil.
2 Cover the chicken and simmer
over a gentle heat for 1¼-1½ hours
until tender, turning it over every
15-20 minutes.
3 Turn off the heat under the pan
and leave the chicken in the cooking
liquid for 1-2 hours until cool.

4 Remove the chicken and cut it into
8 serving pieces, discarding all the
skin and fat. Set the chicken pieces
aside. Strain the cooking liquid and
remove and discard all of the
vegetables, herbs and flavourings.
5 Grind the walnuts in a blender or
food processor, or pound in a mortar
and pestle. Pour 450 ml/¾ pint of
the strained cooking liquid into a
saucepan, add the ground walnuts,
cinnamon and cloves and bring to
the boil over a moderate heat,
stirring. Simmer the mixture for
20 minutes, stirring frequently, until
the sauce thickens. Add salt and
pepper to taste.

6 Add the chicken pieces to the
sauce and heat through for a few
minutes. Carefully lift the chicken out
of the sauce with a slotted spoon
and arrange the pieces on a bed of
rice. Spoon the sauce over the
chicken. Mix the oil with the paprika,
drizzle over the chicken and garnish
with coriander. Serve immediately.

Serves 4
Preparation time: 30 minutes,
plus cooling
Cooking time: 1¾-2 hours

Turkey Mole

This Mexican dish includes an unusual sauce – with chocolate to give it body and richness.

1 x 1-1.25 kg/2-2½ lb boned turkey breast joint
4 tablespoons rapeseed oil
2 bay leaves
2 onions, chopped finely
3 garlic cloves, chopped finely
2 tablespoons sesame seeds
salt and pepper
MOLE SAUCE:
1 x 400 g/14 oz can chopped or crushed tomatoes
25 g/1 oz raisins
25 g/1 oz unblanched almonds, chopped roughly
1 slice of white bread, crusts removed and broken into pieces
1 corn tortilla, broken into pieces (optional)
2 hot fresh green or red chillies, deseeded and chopped roughly
½ teaspoon fennel seeds
½ teaspoon ground cinnamon
¼ teaspoon ground aniseed
¼ teaspoon ground cloves
40 g/1½ oz bitter chocolate, coarsely grated

1 Fry the turkey in 2 tablespoons of oil in a flameproof casserole, turning constantly, for about 10 minutes, until evenly browned. Add the bay leaves, with half the chopped onions and garlic. Cover the turkey with cold water and season to taste.

2 Bring to the boil, cover and simmer gently for about 1½ hours until the turkey is tender.
3 To make the mole sauce, put the remaining onions and garlic in a food processor with all the sauce ingredients, except the chocolate. Process, adding a little turkey liquid to blend the mixture if necessary.
4 When the turkey is cooked, remove it and strain the liquid into a jug. Leave the turkey until cool enough to handle, then shred it. Remove and discard all skin and fat.
5 Heat the remaining oil in the casserole, add the sauce mixture and cook, stirring constantly, for about 5 minutes until dark in colour. Add the chocolate, mix until melted, and gradually add enough cooking

liquid to make a thick, runny sauce. Stir and simmer for 15 minutes until the sauce is rich and dark, adding more of the cooking liquid as necessary. Check seasoning.
6 Heat the turkey in the sauce for about 5 minutes. Meanwhile, put the sesame seeds in a small frying pan and dry-fry over a gentle heat for 2-3 minutes until toasted golden.
7 Serve hot, garnished with toasted sesame seeds. Traditional accompaniments are boiled white rice, tortillas, chopped coriander and fresh chillies, sliced radishes, chopped onions and tomatoes.

Serves 4-6
Preparation time: 30 minutes
Cooking time: 2½-2¾ hours

Chicken and Smoked Ham Gumbo

Gumbo is a kind of soupy stew from Louisiana, usually made with seafood, such as shrimps, crab and scallops. Here it is made with chicken and smoked ham, which is equally delicious. As a variation, you can substitute 375 g/12 oz peeled prawns or 8 scallops for the ham and cook them for just a few minutes.

5 tablespoons rapeseed oil

40 g/1½ oz plain flour

1 large onion, chopped finely

1 red pepper, cored, deseeded and chopped finely

2 garlic cloves, crushed

1.2 litres/2 pints Chicken Stock (see page 8)

1 x 400 g/14 oz can chopped or crushed tomatoes

2 tablespoons chopped fresh parsley

1 tablespoon chopped fresh thyme

¼ teaspoon cayenne pepper

750 g/1½ lb skinned and boned chicken thighs, cut into bite-sized pieces

250 g/8 oz okra, sliced thinly

250 g/8 oz smoked ham in one piece, cut into bite-sized pieces

salt and pepper

chopped spring onions or tiny sprigs of thyme, to garnish (optional)

1 Heat the oil in a large flameproof casserole, sprinkle in the flour and stir well to form a roux. Cook the roux, stirring constantly, over a gentle heat for about 20 minutes until a rich, nutty brown in colour.

2 Add the onion, red pepper and garlic and fry, stirring frequently, for about 5 minutes until softened.

3 Gradually stir in the stock, then add the tomatoes, herbs, cayenne and salt and pepper to taste. Increase the heat and bring to the boil, stirring.

4 Lower the heat and add the chicken and okra. Cover and simmer over a gentle heat, stirring occasionally, for 40 minutes or until the chicken is tender when pierced with a skewer or fork. Add the smoked ham for the last 10 minutes of the cooking time.

5 Adjust the seasoning to taste and serve hot, garnished with spring onions or thyme if liked. Gumbo is traditionally served over boiled rice in soup plates.

Serves 6

Preparation time: 40 minutes

Cooking time: about 1 hour

Cajun Blackened Chicken

125 g/4 oz unsalted butter
6 large skinned chicken breast fillets
50 black peppercorns
10 allspice berries
1 tablespoon cayenne pepper
2 teaspoons garlic salt
lemon wedges, to serve

1 Melt the butter in a saucepan, pour into a bowl and leave to cool.

2 With a sharp knife, score the chicken breasts diagonally in several places. In a mortar and pestle, crush the peppercorns and allspice, then add the cayenne and garlic salt.

3 Rub the spice mixture over the chicken, working it into the slashes in the flesh. Put the chicken in a single layer in a dish and spoon the cooled melted butter over it. Cover and chill in the refrigerator for 2 hours.

4 Heat a heavy-based cast-iron pan over a moderate heat until hot. Add the chicken pieces and cook for

15-20 minutes, turning once, until blackened and tender. Serve hot, garnished with lemon wedges. For a typical Cajun accompaniment, serve with rice mixed with finely chopped green pepper, celery, spring onions and garlic, flavoured with black pepper, cayenne and paprika.

Serves 6
Preparation time: 15 minutes,
plus chilling
Cooking time: 15-20 minutes

Jambalaya

I have substituted mussels for the traditional oysters in this Creole dish from New Orleans. Creole cooking is a mixture of French, Spanish and South American influences.

500 g/1 lb fresh mussels
150 ml/¼ pint dry white wine
150 ml/¼ pint water
1 bouquet garni
2 garlic cloves, crushed
1 x 1.5 kg/3 lb chicken, jointed into
   8 pieces
175 g/6 oz chorizo sausage, chopped
2 tablespoons rapeseed oil
2 onions, chopped finely
2 celery sticks, chopped finely
1 green pepper, cored, deseeded
   and chopped
1 red pepper, cored, deseeded
   and chopped
1 x 400 g/14 oz can chopped tomatoes
1 teaspoon dried thyme
1 teaspoon dried oregano
1 teaspoon cayenne pepper
about 600 ml/1 pint Chicken Stock
   (see page 8) or water
500 g/1 lb long-grain rice
2 bay leaves, broken up
salt and pepper

1 Scrub the mussels with a stiff brush, scraping off the beards and barnacles with a knife. Discard any mussels which remain open.
2 Put the wine, water, bouquet garni, garlic, mussels, and salt and pepper in a large saucepan. Cover tightly with a lid and bring to the boil. Shake the pan vigorously and simmer for 5 minutes until the mussels open. Remove them from the liquid and set aside, discarding any which remain closed. Strain the cooking liquid and reserve.
3 Fry the chicken and chorizo in the oil in a large flameproof casserole, stirring frequently, for 5 minutes. Remove with a slotted spoon and set aside on a plate.
4 Add the onions, celery and peppers to the casserole and fry, stirring constantly, for 5 minutes until softened. Add the tomatoes, thyme, oregano and cayenne and stir. Add the mussel cooking liquid and the stock or water. Bring to the boil, stirring. Stir in the rice and the bay leaves and season to taste.
5 Return the chicken and chorizo and their juices to the casserole, cover and simmer for 40 minutes until the chicken is tender and the rice *al dente*. Add more stock as needed. Discard the bay leaves.
6 Place the mussels on top of the chicken and rice, cover tightly, and heat through for a further 5 minutes. Serve straight from the casserole.

Serves 6
Preparation time: about 40 minutes
Cooking time: about 1 hour

Jamaican Jerk Chicken

Jerk pork is one of Jamaica's most famous national dishes. It is cooked over hot coals at roadside stands all over the island. Here, chicken drumsticks are 'jerked' instead of pork, making perfect outdoor food to eat with your fingers. In winter, it can be cooked under the grill.

2 tablespoons rapeseed oil
1 small onion, chopped finely
10 allspice berries
2 hot red chillies, deseeded and
  chopped roughly

juice of 1 lime
1 teaspoon salt
12 chicken drumsticks

1 Put all of the ingredients, except the chicken drumsticks, in a food processor or spice mill and grind to a paste.
2 Score the chicken drumsticks deeply with a sharp pointed knife, cutting right down as far as the bone.
3 Coat the chicken with the jerk seasoning mixture, brushing it into the slashes in the meat so that the flavour will penetrate. Cover and marinate in the refrigerator overnight.
4 Put the drumsticks on the grid over hot charcoal on the barbecue. Cook, turning frequently, for about 20 minutes until the chicken is charred on the outside and no longer pink on the inside. Serve hot, warm or cold, with ice-cold beer.

Serves 4-6
Preparation time: 15 minutes, plus marinating
Cooking time: about 20 minutes

VARIATION

Oliver's Jerk Chicken

A recipe given to me by a Jamaican friend, whose house I stayed in at Silver Sands, in the north of the island.

1 Replace the drumsticks with a whole 2 kg/4 lb oven-ready chicken, giblets removed, and score the flesh deeply all over.
2 Make the following jerk seasoning: stir together ½ small onion, grated, 2 garlic cloves, crushed, 1 tablespoon ground allspice, 2 teaspoons coarsely ground black pepper, ½ teaspoon dried thyme, ¼ teaspoon each grated nutmeg, ground cinnamon and salt.
3 Coat the chicken with the seasoning and marinate it as for the drumsticks in the main recipe.
4 Barbecue the whole chicken, turning it frequently, for 1¼ hours or until the juices run clear when the thickest part of a thigh is pierced with a skewer or fork. Cut the chicken into pieces to serve.

Serves 4-6
Preparation time: 15 minutes, plus marinating
Cooking time: about 1¼-1½ hours

Nasi Goreng

This famous Indonesian rice dish can be made with different meats besides chicken. Duck or turkey breasts can be used, or pork or beef, or a mixture of different meats. The authentic version includes a nugget of terasi – a dried shrimp paste, mixed in with the onion, garlic and chilli. It is available at oriental speciality shops.

375 g/12 oz long-grain rice
2 eggs
2 tablespoons rapeseed oil
1 small onion, chopped finely
2 garlic cloves, chopped roughly
1 hot fresh red chilli, deseeded and chopped roughly
500 g/1 lb skinned chicken breast fillets, cut diagonally into thin strips
250 g/8 oz peeled cooked prawns
about 2 tablespoons soy sauce
salt and pepper
spring onions, to garnish

1 Rinse rice under running water, put in a large saucepan and cover with cold water. Bring to the boil with 1 teaspoon salt, stir well, lower the heat and simmer, uncovered, for 20 minutes or until rice is *al dente*. Drain, rinse under cold running water, and drain again thoroughly. Set aside to cool.

2 Make an omelette: beat eggs with salt and pepper. Heat 1½ teaspoons oil in a small frying pan until hot but not smoking. Run eggs over base of pan, lift up the edges and let unset egg run underneath. Cook until the underneath is golden and the top set. Slide out of pan, then roll up carefully into a cigar shape. Leave to cool, seam-side down.

3 Crush onion, garlic and chilli (and terasi if using) to a paste, then fry in the remaining oil in a wok or large deep frying pan, for 1-2 minutes until fragrant. Add chicken, and stir-fry for 3-4 minutes until it changes colour on all sides. Add the prawns and 2 tablespoons soy sauce. Stir-fry until the chicken is tender.

4 Mix cold rice with chicken and prawns. Toss over a high heat until rice is piping hot. Add salt, pepper and more soy sauce to taste.

5 Turn rice mixture into a serving dish and garnish with spring onions and the omelette, cut into thin rings. Accompany with prawn crackers.

Serves 4-6
Preparation time: 15 minutes
Cooking time: about 30 minutes

Thai Chicken and Papaya Salad

Papaya is often cooked or served with poultry or meat in Thailand. If papayas are difficult to obtain, mangoes, pineapple or melon can be substituted – a cooling contrast to the spicy dressing.

2 ripe papayas
1 head of crisp lettuce (such as Little Gem or Iceberg), with the leaves separated
½ large cucumber, sliced thinly
50-75 g/2-3 oz bean sprouts
500 g/1 lb skinless chicken breast fillets
rapeseed oil, for brushing

DRESSING:
2 small fresh green or red chillies, cored, deseeded and chopped roughly
2 large garlic cloves, chopped roughly
finely grated zest of 1 lime
juice of 3 limes
2-3 tablespoons fish sauce (nam pla)
2-3 teaspoons brown sugar, to taste

1 First make the dressing. Put the chillies, garlic and lime zest in a mortar and pound with a pestle until crushed to a paste.

2 Stir in the lime juice and fish sauce until evenly mixed with the chilli and garlic paste, then add brown sugar to taste. Cover and set aside while preparing the salad ingredients and cooking the chicken.

3 Peel the papayas, cut each in half lengthways, and scoop out and discard the seeds. Slice the flesh thinly.

4 Arrange the lettuce leaves around the edge of a serving dish, then place the papaya, cucumber and bean sprouts attractively on top.

5 Brush the chicken breasts liberally with oil. Put on the grid over hot charcoal on the barbecue. Cook the chicken for about 7 minutes on each side or until done to your liking. (Alternatively, cook the chicken under a preheated hot grill, or on a cast-iron griddle on top of the stove, for about the same time.)

6 Remove the chicken from the barbecue and place on a board. With a very sharp knife, cut it into diagonal slices across the grain.

7 Arrange the chicken on the serving dish and drizzle over the dressing. Leave to stand for a few minutes before serving.

Serves 4
Preparation time: 30 minutes
Cooking time: 15 minutes

Malaysian Chicken, Noodle and Prawn Stew

The combination of poultry and seafood is very popular in the Far East, and you will find it absolutely delicious. Instead of fish stock, use fish stock cubes, or chicken stock with 1-2 tablespoons of fish sauce added.

4-6 spring onions, shredded
5 cm/2 inch piece of fresh root ginger, cut into very thin matchstick sticks
2 garlic cloves, crushed
2 tablespoons rapeseed oil
375 g/12 oz skinned chicken breast fillets, cut diagonally into thin strips
2 tablespoons rice wine or dry sherry
2 tablespoons soy sauce
1 teaspoon turmeric
1 teaspoon chilli powder
1.8 litres/3 pints fish stock (see introduction above)

125 g/4 oz block creamed coconut, chopped roughly
2 carrots, cut into very thin matchstick strips
250 g/8 oz French beans, cut diagonally into 5-7.5 cm/2-3 inch lengths
125 g/4 oz Chinese egg noodles
125 g/4 oz bean sprouts
8-12 large raw prawns in their shells
salt and pepper

1 Stir-fry the spring onions, ginger and garlic in the oil in a large flameproof casserole for about 5 minutes until softened but not coloured.
2 Add the chicken and stir-fry until it changes colour, then stir in the rice wine or sherry, soy sauce, turmeric, chilli powder and salt and pepper to taste.
3 Gradually add the stock, stirring constantly to mix with the chicken and flavouring ingredients. Add the chopped creamed coconut and simmer, stirring constantly, for about 5 minutes until the coconut has melted.
4 Cover and simmer gently for about 10 minutes until the chicken is just tender.
5 Add the carrots and French beans, cover and simmer for 5 minutes. Add the noodles, bean sprouts and prawns, cover and remove from the heat. Leave to stand for 5 minutes until the noodles are soft and the prawns pink.
6 Remove the prawns from the casserole and pull off their shells with your fingers. Slice the prawns horizontally in half, then return to the casserole and stir well to mix. Adjust the seasoning to taste and serve hot, in warmed bowls.

Serves 6-8
Preparation time: 20 minutes
Cooking time: about 30 minutes

VARIATION

Malaysian Chicken Stew with Spinach and Crab

Replace the French beans with 175 g/6 oz fresh spinach, shredded, and replace the prawns with 250 g/8 oz white crab meat or crab sticks, diced. Proceed as in the main recipe, adding the spinach and crab in step 5 with the noodles and bean sprouts.

Indonesian Chicken and Coconut Curry

1 small onion, chopped roughly

5 cm/2 inch piece of fresh root ginger, chopped roughly

2 garlic cloves, chopped roughly

1 fresh green or red chilli, deseeded and chopped roughly

2 stems of lemon grass, lower part only, sliced

2 tablespoons rapeseed oil

1 teaspoon turmeric

1 kg/2 lb skinned and boned chicken thighs, cut into bite-sized pieces

250 ml/8 fl oz coconut milk

150 ml/¼ pint water

salt

TO FINISH:

50 g/2 oz natural unsalted cashews or macadamia nuts

50 g/2 oz desiccated coconut

1 Crush the onion, ginger, garlic, chilli and lemon grass to a paste.

2 Heat a wok or large deep frying pan until hot. Add the oil and heat over a moderate heat until hot but not smoking. Add the chilli paste and stir-fry over a gentle heat for 1-2 minutes until fragrant.

3 Add the turmeric and stir-fry for 1-2 minutes, then add the chicken, coconut milk and water and bring to the boil over a moderate heat. Stir well to mix, then lower the heat. Cover and simmer gently, stirring frequently, for 40 minutes or until the chicken is tender.

4 Meanwhile, finely chop the cashews or macadamia nuts, or pound them in a mortar and pestle, then place them in a small heavy-bottomed frying pan with the desiccated coconut. Dry-fry over a gentle heat for a few minutes, stirring and tossing the mixture until it is toasted to a rich, nutty brown.

5 When the chicken is tender and the sauce is rich and thick, add salt to taste, then turn the curry into a warmed serving bowl. Sprinkle with the toasted nut and coconut mixture and serve hot. Plain boiled or steamed white rice is the perfect foil for such a rich dish.

Serves 4-6

Preparation time: 30 minutes

Cooking time: about 45 minutes

Hot and Sour Chicken Soup

A soup from China – full of flavour with the slightly chewy dried shiitake mushrooms contrasting with the chicken, fresh ginger and spring onions.

15 g/½ oz dried shiitake mushrooms
2.1 litres/3½ pints Chicken Stock (see page 8)
2 tablespoons soy sauce
2 tablespoons rice wine or dry sherry
1 teaspoon soft brown sugar
1 fresh green chilli, deseeded and chopped very finely
5 cm/2 inch piece of fresh root ginger, shredded very finely
about 250 g/8 oz skinned and boned cooked chicken, shredded finely
6 spring onions, shredded finely
2 carrots, grated
salt and pepper
fresh coriander leaves, to garnish (optional)

1 Soak the dried shiitake mushrooms in warm water to cover for about 20 minutes. Drain and reserve the soaking liquid. Thinly slice the reconstituted mushrooms.
2 Bring the stock to the boil in a large saucepan over a moderate heat. Add the reserved mushroom liquid, the soy sauce, rice wine or sherry, sugar, chilli and ginger. Lower the heat, add the mushrooms and simmer for 20 minutes.

3 Add the chicken, spring onions and carrots and simmer for a further 5 minutes. Add salt and pepper to taste and serve hot, garnished with coriander leaves if you like.

Serves 4-6
Preparation time: 10 minutes, plus soaking
Cooking time: about 25 minutes

Chicken Satay

This popular Indonesian dish, sometimes spelt 'saté', is undoubtedly best cooked over charcoal for a truly authentic flavour, but you can cook it under a preheated hot grill if more convenient. Take care not to overcook the chicken or it will be dry.

4 large skinned chicken breast fillets,
    cut diagonally into thin strips
MARINADE:
¼ onion, grated or chopped very finely
1 garlic clove, crushed
2 teaspoons soft brown sugar
2 tablespoons soy sauce
PEANUT SAUCE:
125 g/4 oz dry roasted peanuts

2 garlic cloves, chopped roughly
1 hot fresh red chilli, deseeded and
    chopped roughly
2.5 cm/1 inch piece of fresh root
    ginger, chopped roughly
300 ml/½ pint canned coconut milk
300 ml/½ pint water
juice of 2 limes
2 teaspoons soft brown sugar

1 To make the marinade, combine the onion, garlic, sugar and soy sauce in a shallow dish. Add the chicken strips and stir well to coat. Cover and marinate for at least 1 hour, or overnight if possible.

2 To make the peanut sauce, put the peanuts in a food processor or blender with the garlic, chilli and ginger, work until finely and evenly ground, then transfer to a saucepan and add the coconut milk, water, lime juice and sugar. Simmer over a moderate heat, stirring frequently, for 10-15 minutes or until a thick sauce is obtained. Remove from the heat.

3 Thirty minutes before cooking the chicken, soak 12 bamboo skewers in warm water to cover. Drain.

4 Thread the chicken strips on to the soaked bamboo skewers. Put the skewers on the grid over hot charcoal on the barbecue. Cook, turning frequently, for 5-8 minutes until the chicken is charred on the outside and no longer pink on the inside.

5 Meanwhile, reheat the peanut sauce and turn into a serving bowl. Serve the satay hot as a starter or snack, with the peanut sauce for dipping. Diced cucumber and compressed rice or bean curd are traditional accompaniments.

Serves 4-6
Preparation time: about 20 minutes, plus marinating
Cooking time: about 30 minutes

VARIATION

Turkey Satay

Replace the chicken with turkey breast fillets and proceed as in the main recipe. For a quick-and-easy satay sauce, put 4 heaped tablespoons crunchy peanut butter in a saucepan with 300 ml/½ pint water, juice of ½ lemon, 1 tablespoon each soy sauce and soft brown sugar and 1 teaspoon chilli powder. Bring to the boil, stirring constantly, then simmer gently for 5 minutes.

Chinese Sweet and Sour Chicken

1 egg
2 tablespoons cornflour
500 g/1 lb skinned chicken breast
    fillets, cut into 2.5 cm/1 inch cubes
rapeseed oil, for deep-frying
salt
coriander, to garnish
SAUCE:
1 teaspoon cornflour
125 ml/4 fl oz cold Chicken Stock
    (see page 8) or water
1 tablespoon soy sauce
1 tablespoon wine or cider vinegar or
    dry sherry
1 tablespoon soft brown sugar
1 tablespoon tomato purée

1 Lightly beat the egg in a shallow dish with the cornflour and a pinch of salt. Add the cubes of chicken and turn them gently to coat with the cornflour mixture. Set aside.
2 To prepare the sauce, blend the cornflour with 2 tablespoons of the stock or water in a jug, then blend in the remaining stock or water and the remaining sauce ingredients. Set the mixture aside.
3 Pour enough oil into a wok for deep-frying and heat to 180-190°C (350-375°F), or until a cube of bread browns in 30 seconds. Deep-fry the cubes of chicken, a few at a time, for 2-3 minutes each batch until golden. Lift out with a slotted spoon and drain on paper towels while deep-frying the remainder.

4 Carefully pour the oil out of the wok and discard. Whisk the sauce again to combine, then pour into the wok. Increase the heat to high and bring to the boil, stirring constantly.
5 Lower the heat and return the chicken to the wok. Simmer over a gentle heat for 30-60 seconds until the chicken is completely heated through. Serve immediately, with plain boiled or steamed white rice or noodles and stir-fried green vegetables, and garnished with coriander sprigs.

Serves 4
Preparation time: 10 minutes
Cooking time: about 10 minutes

Peking Duck

1 x 2 kg/4 lb oven-ready duck
4 tablespoons soft brown sugar
2 tablespoons soy sauce
2 tablespoons clear honey

PANCAKES:

125 g/4 oz plain flour
about 125 ml/4 fl oz boiling water
rapeseed oil, for frying

TO SERVE:

plum or hoisin sauce
½ cucumber, cut into very thin
  matchstick strips
6 spring onions, cut into 5 cm/2 inch
  lengths and shredded finely

1 Remove fat inside the duck. Rinse duck inside and out under cold running water. Pat thoroughly dry, inside and out, with paper towels.
2 Tie string around the neck flap of the duck. Lower the bird into a large saucepan of boiling water for about 1 minute or until the skin is taut.
3 Remove from the water, then hang up by the string over a dish. Leave to dry in a cool airy place for 2 hours.
4 Roast, breast-side up, on a rack in a roasting tin at 190°C (375°F), Gas Mark 5 for 30 minutes.
5 For the pancakes, sift the flour into a bowl, add the boiling water a little at a time, and beat vigorously with a wooden spoon after each addition until a stiff dough is formed. Cover with a cloth and leave to stand for at least 20 minutes.
6 Combine the sugar, soy sauce and honey and brush all over the duck.

Continue roasting 1½ hours or until the skin is crisp, dry and golden.
7 When cooked, transfer duck to a board and let stand for 15 minutes.
8 Make the pancakes: break the dough into 8 pieces with floured hands and roll each into a ball. On a lightly floured surface, roll each ball out to a 15 cm/6 inch round.
9 Heat a little oil in a small frying pan. Add a pancake and fry for 1-2 minutes on each side until puffed up and lightly coloured. Slide on to a warm plate and cover with a damp cloth. Repeat with the remaining pancakes, brushing the pan with more oil between each and stacking them on top of each other under the damp cloth.

10 Remove the string from the duck, slice off the crisp skin and cut it into thin strips. Slice the meat into thin strips. Arrange skin and meat together on a warmed serving plate.
11 Serve the duck with pancakes, plum or hoisin sauce, cucumber and spring onions on separate plates. Put a little sauce on a pancake, add crispy skin, meat, cucumber and spring onions. Roll up and eat with fingers or chopsticks.

Serves 3-4
Preparation time: 45 minutes, plus air-drying
Cooking time: 2 hours
Oven temperature: 190°C (375°F), Gas Mark 5

Chicken Tikka Masala

Chicken Tikka Masala is simply Chicken Tikka cooked in the usual way (see page 97), then simmered briefly in a creamy sauce. It is both mild in flavour and rich and creamy, which makes it one of the most popular dishes in Indian restaurants in the West.

Chicken Tikka (see page 97),
   marinated and threaded on to
   skewers but not cooked
2 tablespoons chopped fresh coriander
juice of ½ lime
MASALA SAUCE:
50 g/2 oz ghee or butter
2 onions, sliced thinly
2.5 cm/1 inch piece of fresh root
   ginger, chopped finely
2 garlic cloves, crushed
6 cardamom pods, bruised

2 teaspoons garam masala
2 teaspoons ground coriander
1 teaspoon chilli powder, or to taste
300 ml/½ pint double cream
2 tablespoons tomato purée
4 tablespoons hot water
½ teaspoon sugar
salt
TO GARNISH:
coriander leaves
slices of lime

1 To make the masala sauce, melt the ghee or butter in a large flameproof casserole, add the onions, ginger and garlic and fry over a gentle heat, stirring frequently, for about 5 minutes, until softened but not coloured.
2 Add the spices and fry, stirring, for 1-2 minutes until fragrant, then add the cream, tomato purée, water, sugar and ½ teaspoon salt. Bring slowly to the boil over a moderate heat, stirring, then lower the heat and simmer gently, stirring occasionally, for 10-15 minutes. Remove the pan from the heat and let stand while cooking the chicken.
3 Barbecue or grill the Chicken Tikka according to the recipe instructions on page 97, then remove the cubes of chicken from the skewers.
4 Add the chicken to the masala sauce, return to a low heat and simmer, stirring, for about 5 minutes. Add the coriander and lime juice and taste for seasoning. Serve immediately, garnished with coriander leaves and slices of lime, and accompanied by plain boiled rice, chapattis or naan bread.

Serves 4
Preparation time: 20 minutes, plus marinating
Cooking time: 40-45 minutes

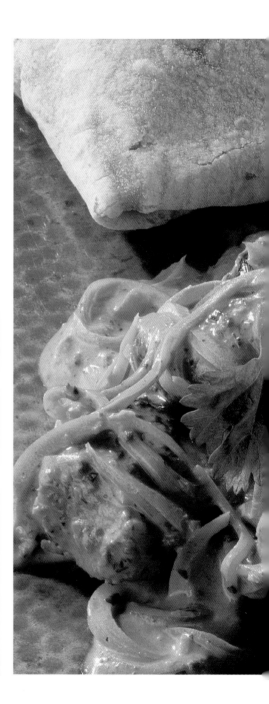

Chicken Korma

Moghul korma dishes from Northern India are rich, creamy and mild in flavour, which is why they are so popular in the West. This recipe is finished off with cream and almonds, making it luxuriously rich.

3 tablespoons ghee or butter
1 onion, chopped finely
2.5 cm/1 inch piece of fresh root ginger, crushed
2 garlic cloves, crushed
5 cm/2 inch cinnamon stick
4 cardamom pods, bruised
4 cloves
2 teaspoons garam masala

1 teaspoon turmeric
½ -1 teaspoon chilli powder, according to taste
12 skinned and boned chicken thighs, cut into bite-sized pieces
300 ml/½ pint double cream
50 g/2 oz ground almonds
salt
toasted flaked almonds, to garnish

1 Melt the ghee or butter in a large flameproof casserole, add the onion, ginger and garlic and fry gently, stirring often, for about 5 minutes until softened but not coloured.

2 Add the whole and ground spices and salt to taste. Fry, stirring, for 1-2 minutes, then add the chicken and stir well to coat in the spice mixture. Increase the heat to moderate and fry, stirring frequently, for about 10 minutes until the chicken changes colour on all sides.

3 Cover the casserole and simmer over a very gentle heat, stirring occasionally, for 20 minutes.

4 Add the cream and ground almonds. Stir well to mix. Simmer uncovered, stirring often, for 10 minutes or until the chicken is tender. If the curry becomes too thick, thin it with a few spoonfuls of water. Remove the whole spices, then taste and add more salt and chilli powder if necessary. Serve hot, garnished with toasted almonds.

Serves 4
Preparation time: 20 minutes
Cooking time: about 40 minutes

Chicken Biryani

For the authentic Indian look and flavour, use basmati rice, with its unique, subtle taste. It is delicate and a little difficult to cook, so do follow these instructions carefully.

50 g/2 oz ghee or butter
1 onion, sliced thinly
2 garlic cloves, crushed
2 teaspoons garam masala
1 teaspoon ground coriander
1 teaspoon chilli powder
1 teaspoon turmeric
500 g/1 lb skinned and boned chicken thighs, cut into small bite-sized pieces
400 ml/14 fl oz cold water
375 g/12 oz basmati rice
6 cardamom pods, bruised
300 ml/½ pint boiling water
salt
fresh coriander leaves, to garnish

1 Melt the ghee or butter in a large flameproof casserole, add the onion and garlic and fry over a gentle heat, stirring frequently, for 5 minutes until softened but not coloured.
2 Sprinkle in the ground spices and salt to taste. Fry gently, stirring, for 1-2 minutes until fragrant, then add the chicken and stir to coat in the spice mixture.
3 Gradually add the cold water, stirring all the time, and bring slowly to the boil over a moderate heat. Lower the heat, cover and simmer, stirring occasionally, for 20 minutes.

4 Meanwhile, rinse the basmati rice in several changes of cold water until the water is almost clear, then put the rice in a medium saucepan with the bruised cardamom pods and ½ teaspoon salt. Pour in the boiling water, then immediately cover the pan with a tight-fitting lid and cook the rice over a gentle heat, without lifting the lid, for 7 minutes.
5 Uncover the rice, fork through very gently, then add to the chicken in the pan and stir gently to mix all the ingredients. Cover and continue cooking over a gentle heat for about 10 minutes longer or until the chicken is tender. Taste and add more salt if necessary.

6 Pile the biryani on to a warmed serving platter, and garnish with coriander leaves. Serve immediately. A plain or cucumber raita would be a good accompaniment, as would a tomato and raw onion sambal.

Serves 4-6
Preparation time: 20 minutes
Cooking time: about 35 minutes

Tandoori Chicken

Instructions are given here for cooking the chicken on the barbecue, for authentic-looking charred chicken, but it can be cooked under the grill. Small clay tandoori ovens are available at specialist kitchenware shops, but they do not achieve the same results as the ones in Indian restaurants which cook at searingly high temperatures.

1 fresh hot red chilli, deseeded and
   chopped roughly
2 garlic cloves, chopped roughly
2.5 cm/1 inch piece of fresh root
   ginger, chopped roughly
2 tablespoons lemon juice
1 tablespoon coriander seeds
1 tablespoon cumin seeds
2 teaspoons garam masala

6 tablespoons natural yogurt
a few drops each of red and yellow
   food colouring
4 skinned chicken portions
salt

TO GARNISH:
lemon wedges
coriander sprigs

1 Put the chilli, garlic, ginger and lemon juice in an electric spice mill with the whole spices and garam masala and work to a paste.
2 Transfer the spice paste to a shallow dish in which the chicken portions will fit in a single layer. Add the yogurt, food colouring and ½ teaspoon salt and stir well to mix. Set aside.
3 Score the flesh of the chicken deeply with a sharp pointed knife, cutting right down as far as the bone. Put the chicken in a single layer in the dish, then spoon the marinade over the chicken and brush it into the cuts in the flesh. Cover and marinate in the refrigerator for at least 4 hours, but preferably overnight.
4 Put the chicken on the grid over hot charcoal on the barbecue. Cook, turning often, for 30 minutes or until the juices run clear when pierced with a skewer or fork. Serve hot, garnished with lemon wedges and coriander sprigs, and accompanied by a salad of shredded lettuce, white cabbage and raw onion slices, a sauce made of yogurt and chopped mint, and plain or garlic naan bread.

Serves 4
Preparation time: 20 minutes, plus marinating
Cooking time: 40 minutes

VARIATION
Chicken Tikka

Replace the chicken portions with 4 large skinned and boned chicken breasts, cut into cubes, and proceed as in the main recipe. After marinating, thread the cubes of chicken on to kebab skewers. Place the skewers on the grid over hot charcoal on the barbecue (or under the grill) and cook, turning the skewers often, for 10-15 minutes until the chicken juices run clear.

Balti Chicken

*Balti dishes from Northern
India are named after the vessel
in which they are cooked — a
metal pot, rather like a wok.*

½ teaspoon black peppercorns
½ teaspoon nigella seeds
½ teaspoon fennel seeds
2 tablespoons rapeseed oil
1 onion, sliced thinly
2.5 cm/1 inch piece of fresh root
    ginger, crushed
1 garlic clove, crushed
1 tablespoon garam masala
1 teaspoon ground coriander
1 teaspoon ground cumin
1 teaspoon chilli powder, or to taste
1 teaspoon turmeric
475 ml/16 fl oz water
50 g/2 oz coconut milk powder
1 tablespoon lemon juice
6 cardamom pods, bruised
5 cm/2 inch cinnamon stick
1 bay leaf
1 kg/2 lb skinned and boned chicken
    thighs, cut into bite-sized pieces
4 ripe tomatoes, skinned, deseeded and
    chopped roughly
¼ teaspoon sugar
salt
fresh coriander leaves, to garnish

1 Dry-fry the peppercorns, nigella
and fennel seeds in a wok or large
deep frying pan over a gentle heat,
stirring constantly, for 2-3 minutes
until fragrant, then pound to a fine
powder in a mortar and pestle.

2 Heat the oil in the same pan, add
the onion, ginger and garlic and fry
gently, stirring frequently, for about
5 minutes until soft but not coloured.
3 Add the toasted spices, garam
masala, coriander, cumin, chilli
powder and turmeric. Stir-fry for
2-3 minutes, then add the water,
coconut milk powder, lemon juice
and ½ teaspoon salt. Bring to the
boil, stirring, then add the
cardamoms, cinnamon and bay leaf.
Simmer, stirring occasionally, for
15-20 minutes, until a glaze forms
on top of the liquid.

4 Add the chicken, tomatoes and
sugar and stir well. Cover and cook
over a gentle heat for 30 minutes or
until the chicken is tender when
pierced with a fork or skewer.
5 Remove and discard the bay leaf
and cinnamon stick, then taste, and
add more salt if necessary. Serve
hot, sprinkled with fresh coriander
leaves, and accompanied by
chapattis, puris or naan bread.

Serves 4-6
Preparation time: 30 minutes
Cooking time: 40 minutes

Chicken Jalfrezi

Chicken Jalfrezi is an Indian curry with a strong flavour of coriander, from both the spice and the herb. It is intended to be red hot, but you can reduce the amount of chillies or omit the chilli seeds.

2 tablespoons rapeseed oil

1 onion, chopped finely

5 cm/2 inch piece of fresh root ginger, crushed

1 garlic clove, crushed

2 red hot chillies, chopped very finely

2 teaspoons garam masala

2 teaspoons ground coriander

6 ripe tomatoes, peeled, deseeded and chopped roughly

1 tablespoon tomato purée

2 teaspoons lemon juice

¼ teaspoon sugar

450 ml/¾ pint Chicken Stock (see page 8)

1 kg/2 lb skinned, boned chicken thighs, cut into bite-sized pieces

1 large green pepper, cored, deseeded and chopped

2 tablespoons chopped fresh coriander

salt

1 Heat the oil in a large flameproof casserole, add the onion, ginger and garlic and fry over a gentle heat, stirring frequently, for 5 minutes until softened but not coloured.
2 Add the chillies, garam masala and ground coriander and fry, stirring constantly, for 2-3 minutes to release the aroma of the spices. Add the tomatoes, tomato purée, lemon juice, sugar and ½ teaspoon salt. Stir well to mix, then pour in the stock and bring to the boil over a moderate heat, stirring all the time. Simmer for about 15 minutes until thickened and reduced.
3 Add the chicken, cover and simmer over a gentle heat, stirring occasionally, for 30 minutes.
4 Add the chopped green pepper and the chopped fresh coriander and simmer for a further 10 minutes or until the chicken is tender when pierced with a skewer or fork. Check seasoning, and serve hot, with boiled rice or chapattis, yogurt and cucumber raita and mango chutney, or with sliced bananas and toasted desiccated coconut.

Serves 4-6
Preparation time: 20 minutes
Cooking time: 50-55 minutes

Chicken Dhansak

Dhansak recipes originated in Persia although they are now more usually associated with Indian cuisine. They always include lentils among their ingredients and the chicken is always served off the bone, together with saffron or pilau rice.

250 g/8 oz yellow split lentils
900 ml/1½ pints water
2 tablespoons ghee or butter
4 skinned chicken portions
1 large onion, chopped finely
2 garlic cloves, chopped finely
2 teaspoons garam masala

1 teaspoon turmeric
1 teaspoon hot chilli powder
½ teaspoon ground cloves
4 large ripe tomatoes, skinned, deseeded and chopped roughly
salt

1 Put lentils and water in a large saucepan, add 1 teaspoon salt and bring to the boil over a moderate heat. Lower the heat, cover and simmer gently for 30 minutes or until lentils are tender and have absorbed most of the water.
2 Meanwhile, melt the ghee or butter in a large flameproof casserole, add the chicken and sauté for 7-10 minutes over a moderate heat until golden on all sides. Remove with a slotted spoon and set aside on a plate.
3 Add the onion, garlic and spices to the casserole and fry over a gentle heat, stirring frequently, for about 5 minutes until softened. Add the tomatoes and salt to taste and stir well to mix. Return the chicken to the casserole with the juices that have collected on the plate and spoon over the vegetables.
4 When the lentils are cooked, pour them over the chicken and shake the casserole vigorously so that they mix into the spiced vegetables. Add a little water if the mixture seems dry. Cover and simmer over a gentle heat, stirring occasionally, for 30 minutes, or until the chicken is tender when pierced with a skewer or fork.
5 Remove the casserole from the heat. Lift the chicken out of the lentil mixture and leave until cool enough to handle.
6 Remove the chicken from the bones and cut the meat into bite-sized pieces. Return the chicken to the casserole and reheat for 5 minutes or so. Taste, and add salt if necessary. Serve hot, with saffron rice.

Serves 4
Preparation time: 20 minutes
Cooking time: about 1 hour

VARIATION

Chicken Curry with Chick Peas and Potatoes

Make the curry according to the main recipe, but with the following differences: omit the lentils. Replace the chicken portions with 1 kg/2 lb skinned and boned chicken thighs, cut into bite-sized pieces. Proceed as in the main recipe, adding a 400 g/14 oz can chick peas, drained, and 2 medium potatoes, cut into chunks, with the tomatoes in step 3. Proceed as in the main recipe, omitting steps 5 and 6. Adjust the seasoning to taste, then serve.

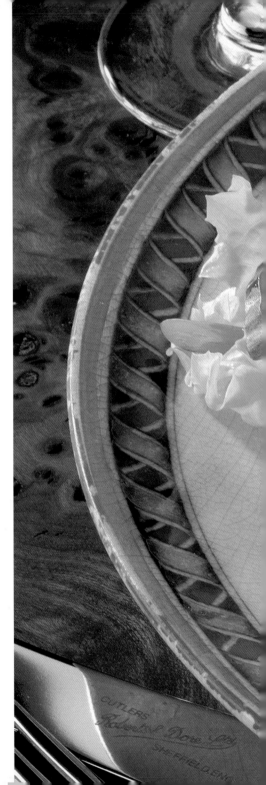

Chicken with Oyster Mushrooms, Garlic and Cream

Delicate oyster mushrooms are excellent for sauce making.

125 g/4 oz smoked streaky bacon rashers, rinds removed, cut into strips
15 g/½ oz butter
6 large skinned chicken breast fillets
1 tablespoon plain flour
300 ml/½ pint dry white wine
175 g/6 oz fresh oyster mushrooms, sliced thinly
1 garlic clove, crushed
75 ml/3 fl oz crème fraîche
½ teaspoon chopped fresh rosemary or ¼ teaspoon dried
salt and pepper
fresh rosemary, to garnish

1 Fry the strips of bacon gently in a large flameproof casserole, stirring, for about 5 minutes until the fat runs. Add the butter and, when melted, sauté the chicken over a moderate heat for about 5 minutes until golden on all sides.
2 Sprinkle in the flour and turn the chicken to coat, then gradually stir in the wine and bring to the boil, stirring. Add the mushrooms, garlic and crème fraîche with the rosemary and plenty of pepper.
3 Stir well, then cover and simmer gently for 25 minutes or until the chicken is tender when pierced with a skewer or fork. Turn and baste it frequently.
4 Taste the sauce for seasoning. Serve hot, garnished with fresh rosemary. New potatoes tossed in chopped fresh herbs would go well with this dish, together with a crisp green salad.

Serves 6
Preparation time: 20 minutes
Cooking time: about 30 minutes

Vegetable Terrine with Chicken Mousseline

This delicately flavoured dish creates a stunning impression.

500 g/1 lb skinned chicken breast
   fillets, chopped roughly
2 eggs, beaten lightly
175 ml/6 fl oz double cream
¼-½ teaspoon Tabasco sauce
about 30 young spinach leaves, with
   any tough stalks removed
175 g/6 oz French beans, topped
   and tailed
3 large carrots, cut into very thin
   matchstick strips
250 g/8 oz frozen peas
salt and pepper

1 To make the mousseline, purée the chicken in a food processor, add the eggs, cream, Tabasco and salt and pepper to taste, and purée again.
2 Blanch the spinach leaves for 10 seconds in a large saucepan of lightly salted boiling water. Remove the leaves with a large slotted spoon and reserve the water. Cool the leaves quickly under cold running water, separate them carefully and leave to dry on a clean tea towel.
3 Blanch the beans, carrots and peas separately in the spinach blanching water, allowing only 2 minutes for each vegetable. Remove as before, refresh under cold running water and dry thoroughly on a clean tea towel.
4 Line the bottom and sides of a 1 kg/2 lb loaf tin with three-quarters of the spinach leaves.
5 Spoon one-quarter of the mousseline into the tin and smooth the surface. Place the beans closely, lengthways, over the mousseline.
6 Spoon in another quarter of the mousseline and arrange the carrot sticks lengthways on top. Repeat with more mousseline and the peas, then top with the remaining mousseline. Cover with the rest of the spinach leaves.
7 Cover the loaf tin with foil and place in a roasting tin. Pour in enough hot water to come halfway up the sides of the loaf tin. Place in a preheated oven, 190°C (375°F), Gas Mark 5 for 1¼ hours.
8 Remove the loaf tin from the water and leave the terrine to cool. Chill for at least 4 hours before serving.

Serves 8
Preparation time: about 1 hour, plus cooling and chilling
Cooking time: 1¼ hours
Oven temperature: 190°C (375°F), Gas Mark 5

Chicken Cordon Bleu

A classic dish, available in most supermarkets – but surprisingly easy to make yourself.

4 large skinned chicken breast fillets
4 thin slices of smoked ham
4 thin slices of Gruyère or
  Emmental cheese
20 g/¾ oz plain flour
1 egg, beaten
75 g/3 oz dried breadcrumbs
3 tablespoons rapeseed oil
salt and pepper
TO SERVE:
lemon wedges and parsley
  sprigs (optional)

1 Make a long horizontal slit through the thickest part of each chicken breast without cutting right through. Open out and place between 2 sheets of greaseproof paper. Pound each chicken breast with a rolling pin until thin.

2 Season each breast, then place a slice of smoked ham on one side of each and top with a slice of cheese, cutting them to fit if necessary.

3 Fold the breasts over to reshape the fillets and secure with wooden cocktail sticks.

4 Spread seasoned flour on one plate, breadcrumbs on another, and pour beaten egg on a third.

5 Coat each chicken breast – first in the flour, then in beaten egg, and then in the breadcrumbs, pressing them on firmly so that they stick. Chill for 1 hour.

6 Heat the oil in a frying pan large enough to hold the chicken in a single layer. Add the chicken and shallow fry for 10 minutes on each side, turning once, until crisp and golden. Remove with a slotted spoon and drain on paper towels. Remove the cocktail sticks and discard. Serve hot, garnished with lemon wedges and parsley sprigs if liked, accompanied by French fries and a green salad.

Serves 4
Preparation time: 30 minutes, plus chilling
Cooking time: 20 minutes

Chicken Suprêmes with Roast Peppers

Roasting the peppers under the grill gives them a wonderful smoky flavour – a barbecue will make them taste even smokier.

4 sweet peppers in different colours
3 tablespoons extra-virgin olive oil
4 skinned chicken suprêmes or
   part-boned chicken breasts
1 onion, sliced thinly
2 garlic cloves, crushed

50 g/2 oz sun-dried tomatoes in oil,
   sliced thinly
2 teaspoons chopped fresh basil
a few tablespoons dry white wine
salt and pepper
basil sprigs, to garnish

1 Roast the peppers under a hot grill, turning frequently, for about 15 minutes until the skins blacken and blister on all sides. Remove from the grill and place each one immediately in a plastic bag. Tie each bag securely, then leave until the peppers are completely cold – at least 4 hours or overnight.

2 Unwrap the peppers and, one by one, hold under cold running water and rub off the blackened skins with your fingers. Pull off the stalks, slit open the peppers and remove the cores and seeds. Pat the peppers thoroughly dry with paper towels, then cut them lengthways into thin strips with a sharp knife.

3 Heat the oil in a large sauté pan, and sauté the chicken over a moderate heat for 7-10 minutes until golden. Remove and set aside on a plate.

4 Add the onion slices to the pan and fry over a gentle heat, stirring frequently, for about 5 minutes until softened but not coloured.

5 Add the roasted pepper strips, garlic, the sun-dried tomatoes, basil and salt and pepper to taste. Stir well to mix, and moisten with wine. Return the chicken to the pan with the juices that have collected on the plate and spoon the pepper mixture over the top. Cover and cook for 20 minutes or until the chicken is tender when pierced with a skewer or fork, turning the chicken over and basting with the cooking liquid frequently during this time.

6 Adjust the seasoning to taste and serve hot, garnished with basil sprigs. Polenta (boiled, grilled or fried) would make the perfect accompaniment, followed by a simple green salad tossed in a dressing made with olive oil and balsamic vinegar.

Serves 4
Preparation time: 30 minutes, plus cooling
Cooking time: about 45 minutes

Normandy Chicken

Granny Smith apples are best for this dish – their tart flavour is delicious with the cider and cream. Don't slice the apples until you are ready to cook them or they will turn brown.

1 tablespoon extra-virgin olive oil
40 g/1½ oz butter
6 skinned part-boned chicken breasts
1 onion, chopped finely
4 dessert apples, peeled, cored
  and sliced
1 teaspoon soft brown sugar
500 ml/17 fl oz dry cider
1 bay leaf
175 ml/6 fl oz double cream
salt and pepper
TO FINISH:
15 g/½ oz butter
¼ teaspoon soft brown sugar
2 dessert apples, peeled, cored
  and sliced
6 tablespoons double cream
fresh bay leaves (optional)

1 Heat the olive oil and butter in a large flameproof casserole, add the chicken, in batches if necessary, and sauté over a moderate heat for 7-10 minutes until golden on all sides. Remove with a slotted spoon and drain on paper towels.
2 Add the onion to the casserole and fry gently, stirring frequently, for about 5 minutes until softened but not coloured. Add the apple slices and sugar and stir to mix with the onion. Add 300 ml/½ pint of the cider, the bay leaf and salt and pepper to taste. Bring to the boil, stirring, then simmer for 15-20 minutes until the apples are softened.
3 Mash the apples into the liquid with a potato masher or wooden spoon, leaving some chunks of apple to give texture. Stir in the remaining cider and bring to the boil.
4 Add the chicken, cover and simmer gently for 30 minutes or until tender when pierced with a skewer or fork, turning the chicken over and basting with the sauce frequently during this time.
5 Add the cream, stir into the sauce, then heat gently for 1-2 minutes.

Discard the bay leaf and taste the sauce for seasoning. Remove from the heat and let stand, covered, while preparing the garnish.
6 Melt the butter and sugar in a frying pan, add the apple slices and toss to coat. Fry gently, stirring, for about 5 minutes until just softened.
7 Transfer the chicken and sauce to a warmed serving platter. Arrange apple slices over the chicken, drizzle each portion with 1 tablespoon cream and garnish with fresh bay leaves, if using. Serve hot, with warm French bread or garlic bread and a crisp green salad.

Serves 6
Preparation time: about 30 minutes
Cooking time: 1-1¼ hours

Spiced Roast Chicken

In this Indian-inspired dish, the spiced yogurt forms a dark, crisp crust contrasting with the moist and succulent white meat.

2 garlic cloves, chopped roughly

2.5 cm/1 inch piece of fresh root ginger, chopped roughly

1-2 dried red chillies, chopped roughly

1 tablespoon cumin seeds

1 x 500 g/1 lb carton natural yogurt

2 teaspoons turmeric

1 teaspoon dried mint

½ teaspoon ground mixed spice

1 x 2 kg/4 lb oven-ready chicken, giblets removed

⅓ cucumber, cut into very thin matchstick strips

2 tablespoons chopped fresh mint

salt

mint sprigs, to garnish

1 Put the garlic, ginger, chillies and cumin seeds in a food processor with about half the yogurt, the turmeric, dried mint, mixed spice and ½ teaspoon salt. Work until all the ingredients are finely ground and evenly mixed into the yogurt – the mixture will be quite runny.

2 Wash inside the chicken and dry thoroughly with paper towels. Slash the skin through to the flesh with a sharp pointed knife, then truss the chicken with string.

3 Put the bird into a large bowl and pour the yogurt mixture all over. Cover and leave to marinate for at least 8 hours or overnight, turning the chicken from time to time.

4 Put the chicken in an ovenproof dish into which it just fits. Place in a preheated oven, 180°C (350°F), Gas Mark 4 for 2-2¼ hours or until the juices run clear when the thickest part of a thigh is pierced with a skewer or fork. Baste frequently and spoon over half the remaining yogurt halfway through the roasting time.

5 Remove the bird, cover tightly with foil and set aside to rest in a warm place. Keep the cooking juices hot.

6 Make a simple cucumber raita by mixing the remaining yogurt with the cucumber, chopped fresh mint and salt to taste. Turn into a serving bowl.

7 Remove the trussing string and discard. Put the chicken on a warmed serving platter and, if liked, pour on some or all of the cooking juices, or pour them into a small jug to be served separately. Garnish the chicken with mint and serve immediately, with the cucumber raita. Basmati rice would make another ideal accompaniment, with a dish of curried vegetables, and a sambal salad of diced beetroot, onion and a little yogurt.

Serves 4

Preparation time: 15 minutes, plus marinating

Cooking time: 2-2¼ hours

Oven temperature: 180°C (350°F), Gas Mark 4

Chicken with White Wine, Cream and Tarragon

Chicken poached gently with white wine, stock and tarragon is both moist and full of flavour. If you like, you can add a knob of unsalted butter at the end to further enrich the sauce.

600 ml/1 pint well-flavoured Chicken
   Stock (see page 8)
200 ml/7 fl oz dry white wine
8 tarragon sprigs

4 skinned, part-boned chicken breasts
250 ml/8 fl oz double cream
good pinch of mustard powder
salt and pepper

1 Pour the chicken stock and wine into a large flameproof casserole, add 2 of the tarragon sprigs and salt and pepper to taste and bring to a simmer.
2 Add the chicken, cover and simmer over a gentle heat for 20-25 minutes or until just tender when pierced with a skewer or fork, turning the chicken over occasionally during this time.
3 Remove the chicken with a slotted spoon and set aside on a plate. Strip the leaves from 2 of the remaining tarragon sprigs and chop finely.
4 Pour the cream into the casserole. Increase the heat and bring to the boil, stirring all the time, then simmer, stirring frequently, for about 15 minutes until reduced by about one-third.
5 Lower the heat, add the chopped tarragon and mustard powder and stir to mix, then add the chicken with the juices that have collected on the plate. Heat through for 5 minutes, basting the chicken frequently with the sauce. Adjust the seasoning to taste.
6 Serve hot, garnished with the remaining tarragon sprigs. Steamed or boiled rice, pressed into timbale shapes, would make an appropriate accompaniment, so too would a delicate green vegetable, such as mangetout or fine French beans.

Serves 4
Preparation time: 10 minutes
Cooking time: 30 minutes

VARIATION

Chicken with Champagne and Cream Sauce

Another dish with wine and cream, where the chicken is sautéed before poaching.

1 Sauté 4 skinned, part-boned chicken breasts in 50 g/2 oz butter over a moderate heat in a flameproof casserole for about 7-10 minutes until golden.
2 Gently warm 4 tablespoons Cognac in a small saucepan, pour over the chicken and set alight. When the flames have died down, add 200 ml/7 fl oz chicken stock, 2 tarragon sprigs, salt and pepper. Cover and simmer gently for 20 minutes, turning and basting often, until the chicken is tender. Set the chicken aside on a plate.
3 Pour 200 ml/7 fl oz Champagne brut into the casserole, add 1 tablespoon tomato purée and 125 ml/4 fl oz crème fraîche. Bring to the boil, reduce the heat, and simmer for about 5 minutes until thickened and reduced. Discard the tarragon and return the chicken to the sauce. Serve, garnished with fresh tarragon.

Serves 4
Preparation time: 15 minutes
Cooking time: about 40 minutes

Chicken Breasts en Croûte

2 tablespoons extra-virgin olive oil

125 g/4 oz brown cap mushrooms, chopped finely

2 garlic cloves, crushed

2 teaspoons chopped fresh thyme or 1 teaspoon dried

6 large skinned chicken breast fillets

125 g/4 oz pâté de campagne

2 tablespoons sherry or brandy

1 x 425 g/14 oz packet frozen puff pastry, thawed

salt and pepper

beaten egg, to glaze

TO GARNISH:

sautéed mushroom slices

thyme sprigs

1 Heat the oil in a small frying pan, add the mushrooms and sauté over a moderate heat, stirring frequently, for about 5 minutes until the juices run.

2 Increase the heat to high and stir the mushrooms until all of the liquid has evaporated and the mushrooms are quite dry.

3 Add the garlic, thyme and salt and pepper to taste and cook for a further 5 minutes. Remove from the heat and leave to cool.

4 Make a long horizontal slit through the thickest part of each chicken breast without cutting right through.

5 Soften the pâté in a bowl with the sherry or brandy, then beat in the mushroom mixture until evenly combined. Spread the pâté inside the cavities in the chicken breasts, dividing it equally between them, then close the chicken tightly around the stuffing.

6 Roll out the pastry on a floured work surface and cut out 6 squares large enough to enclose the chicken breasts. Brush the edges of the pastry with water.

7 Place a stuffed chicken breast in the centre of each pastry square, then bring up the pastry around the chicken to form a parcel. Brush the seams with more water and press together well to seal.

8 Put the chicken parcels, seam-side down, on a moistened baking sheet. Roll out the pastry trimmings and cut small decorative shapes. Brush the parcels all over with beaten egg, then press decorative shapes on top. Brush the shapes with beaten egg.

9 Place in a preheated oven, 200°C (400°F), Gas Mark 6 for 30 minutes or until the pastry is golden and the chicken feels tender when pierced in the centre with a skewer. Serve hot, garnished with a few sautéed mushroom slices and thyme sprigs. A juicy vegetable dish, such as ratatouille, would make a good accompaniment, as would new potatoes, boiled or steamed in their skins and tossed in butter or olive oil and chopped fresh herbs.

Serves 6

Preparation time: 30 minutes

Cooking time: about 40 minutes

Oven temperature: 200°C (400°F), Gas Mark 6

Roast Duck with Fresh Orange and Cointreau Sauce

1 x 2.75-3.25 kg/5½-6½ lb oven-ready
  duck, giblets removed
2 teaspoons plain flour
150 ml/¼ pint Chicken Stock (see
  page 8)
finely grated zest of 1 large orange
juice of 2 large oranges
3 tablespoons Cointreau or other
  orange-flavoured liqueur
salt and pepper
TO GARNISH:
fresh orange slices
fresh watercress or bay leaves

1 Weigh the duck and calculate the cooking time, allowing 25 minutes per 500 g/1 lb.
2 Pat the bird dry inside and out with paper towels. Put the duck, breast-side up, on a rack in a roasting tin. Prick the skin all over with a skewer or fork and then rub all over with salt.
3 Place in a preheated oven, 190°C (375°F), Gas Mark 5 for the calculated cooking time, increasing the temperature to 200°C (400°F), Gas Mark 6 for the last 10 minutes.
4 Remove the duck from the rack, place on a warmed serving platter and cover tightly with foil. Set aside to rest in a warm place while making the sauce.
5 Pour off all but about 1 tablespoon fat from the roasting tin and set the tin on top of the stove. Sprinkle in the flour and cook over a gentle heat, stirring, for 1-2 minutes until golden. Gradually stir in the stock and bring to the boil over a moderate heat, stirring all the time. Lower the heat, add the orange zest and juice, the Cointreau and salt and pepper to taste. Simmer, stirring, for a few minutes or so until the sauce thickens. Taste for seasoning, then pour into a warmed sauce boat.
6 Serve the duck whole, garnished with orange slices and a bouquet of fresh watercress or sprigs of fresh bay leaves. Serve the sauce separately. A dish of creamed potatoes or gratin dauphinois would be a perfect accompaniment, as would a seasonal green vegetable, such as mangetout or broccoli.

Serves 4
Preparation time: 30 minutes
Cooking time: about 2½ hours
Oven temperature: 190°C (375°F), Gas Mark 5, then 200°C (400°F), Gas Mark 6

Duck Terrine with Cherries, Green Peppercorns and Lime

1 x 3 kg/6 lb duck
4 tablespoons kirsch
750 g/1½ lb belly of pork, chopped roughly
125 g/4 oz crustless bread, torn into pieces
finely grated zest and juice of 2 limes

2 tablespoons green peppercorns, crushed lightly
375 g/12 oz streaky bacon rashers, rinds removed
1 x 400 g/14 oz can stoned cherries, drained
salt and pepper

1 Bone the duck and discard skin and fat. Chop all the meat, except the breast.
2 Slice the breast thinly, place in a dish and sprinkle with kirsch. Set aside.
3 Purée the chopped duck and belly of pork coarsely in a food processor with the bread. Turn the mixture into a bowl, and stir in the lime zest and juice, the peppercorns and salt and pepper to taste.
4 Stretch the bacon with the flat of the blade of a large chef's knife. Line the base and sides of a 20 cm/8 inch round cake tin with about three-quarters of the rashers.
5 Spread half the terrine mixture in the tin, then arrange the kirsch-soaked slices of breast in a single layer on top and dot the cherries in between.
6 Cover with the remaining terrine mixture and level the surface. Press down firmly, then cover with the remaining bacon rashers.
7 Cover the cake tin with foil, place in a roasting tin, and pour in enough hot water to come halfway up the sides of the cake tin. Cook in a preheated oven, 180°C (350°F), Gas Mark 4 for 2½ hours.
8 Remove the cake tin from the water and slowly drain off the excess fat from the terrine. Cover with clean foil, put a plate and some heavy weights on top and leave in a cold place overnight.
9 The next day, carefully turn the terrine out on to a board or plate. Remove any sediment and jelly from the bacon with a knife and paper towels, then chill the terrine in the refrigerator for at least 4 hours before serving. Cut into slices and serve with fresh crusty bread.

Serves 12
Preparation time: about 1 hour, plus cooling and chilling
Cooking time: 2½ hours
Oven temperature: 180°C (350°F), Gas Mark 4

VARIATION

Duck Terrine en Croûte

1 After removing the sediment and jelly from the weighted terrine in Step 9 of the main recipe, roll out 250 g/8 oz ready-made puff pastry on a lightly floured surface, into a round large enough to wrap around the terrine.
2 Place the terrine in the centre of the pastry and brush all around the edge of the pastry with beaten egg. Wrap the terrine in the pastry, then place seam-side down on a dampened baking sheet. Brush all over with more beaten egg, then make decorative shapes out of the pastry trimmings, press on to the top, and brush with beaten egg.
3 Place in a preheated oven, 200°C (400°F), Gas Mark 6, for 25 minutes or until golden. Cool before serving.

Serves 6
Preparation time: 1¼ hours, plus cooling
Cooking time: about 3 hours

Chicken Kiev

4 large skinned chicken breast fillets
20 g/¾ oz plain flour
2 eggs, beaten
125 g/4 oz dried white breadcrumbs
rapeseed oil, for deep-frying
salt and pepper
GARLIC BUTTER:
125 g/4 oz unsalted butter, softened
4 garlic cloves, crushed
2 tablespoons finely chopped
fresh parsley
TO GARNISH:
lemon wedges and parsley
sprigs (optional)

1 First make the garlic butter. Beat the butter with the garlic, parsley and salt and pepper to taste. Shape the garlic butter into a rectangle on a sheet of non-stick baking parchment, then wrap and place in the freezer for at least 1 hour or until firm.

2 Put the chicken breasts between 2 sheets of greaseproof paper and pound until thin with a rolling pin.
3 Unwrap the garlic butter and cut it into 4 sticks. Put 1 stick in the centre of each chicken breast, then roll the chicken around the stick, folding in the sides so the butter is completely enclosed. If necessary, secure with wooden cocktail sticks.
4 Spread the flour out on a plate and season with salt and pepper to taste. Spread the beaten eggs on a second plate, and the breadcrumbs on a third.
5 Coat the chicken breasts first in the seasoned flour, then in the beaten eggs, and then in the breadcrumbs. Press the breadcrumbs on firmly so that they stick. Repeat to give a second coating of egg and breadcrumbs (this is important: it helps to insulate the garlic butter so that the heat from the oil does not

penetrate too early and melt the butter before the chicken is cooked). Chill for at least 1 hour.
6 Heat the oil in a deep-fat fryer to 180-190°C (350-375°F), or until a cube of bread browns in 30 seconds. Carefully lower the chicken parcels into the hot oil and deep-fry for 7-10 minutes until the breadcrumbs are golden brown and crisp on all sides, turning the chicken very carefully halfway through. Remove with a slotted spoon and drain on paper towels. Remove and discard the cocktail sticks. Serve hot, garnished with lemon and parsley if liked, and accompanied by a salad of mixed green leaves, such as frisée, rocket and lamb's lettuce.

Serves 4
Preparation time: 30 minutes, plus freezing and chilling
Cooking time: 7-10 minutes

Chicken with White Wine, Gruyère and Mushrooms

4 skinned, part-boned chicken breasts
50 g/2 oz unsalted butter
½ teaspoon dried mixed herbs
½ teaspoon dried tarragon
250 g/8 oz button mushrooms,
    sliced thinly
25 g/1 oz plain flour
300 ml/½ pint milk
150 ml/¼ pint dry white wine
75 ml/3 fl oz double cream
125 g/4 oz Gruyère cheese, grated
good pinch of freshly grated nutmeg
salt and pepper

1 Put the chicken breasts in a single layer in an ovenproof dish, dot with half the butter, sprinkle with the herbs, and season to taste. Cover with foil and place in a preheated oven, 180°C (350°F), Gas Mark 4 for 30 minutes, or until just tender when pierced with a skewer or fork.
2 Meanwhile, melt the remaining butter in a saucepan, add the mushrooms and sauté over a moderate heat, stirring frequently, for about 5 minutes until the juices run.
3 Sprinkle in the flour and cook, stirring, for 1-2 minutes. Remove the pan from the heat and add the milk a little at a time, beating vigorously with a balloon whisk or wooden spoon after each addition. Add the wine in the same way.
4 Return the pan to the heat and bring to the boil, stirring all the time. Lower the heat and simmer, stirring, for about 5 minutes until thickened.
5 Add the cream, two-thirds of the Gruyère, the nutmeg and salt and pepper to taste, and simmer very gently for a further 5 minutes. Remove from the heat.
6 When the chicken is tender, remove from the oven and increase the oven heat to maximum. Tip any juices from the chicken into the sauce and stir well to mix. Pour the sauce over the chicken in the dish and sprinkle with the remaining Gruyère.
7 Return the chicken to the oven and bake for a further 5 minutes, or until golden and bubbling. Serve hot, with a salad of crisp green leaves, finely sliced roasted peppers and sun-dried tomatoes.

Serves 4
Preparation time: 30 minutes
Cooking time: about 35 minutes
Oven temperature: 180°C (350°F), Gas Mark 4, then 240°C (475°F), Gas Mark 9

Duck Breasts with Spicy Mango Relish

Hot crispy duck with sweet and spicy mango relish makes an easy dish for entertaining. The relish can be made the day before, so all you have to do is roast the duck quickly in the oven before serving.

6 duck breast fillets, each
    about 175 g/6 oz
salt
coriander sprigs, to garnish (optional)
MANGO RELISH:
3 ripe mangoes
1 tablespoon rapeseed oil

1 small onion, chopped finely
2.5 cm/1 inch piece of fresh root
    ginger, crushed
1 garlic clove, crushed
2 teaspoons dark brown sugar
¼ teaspoon cayenne pepper
2 tablespoons chopped fresh coriander

1 To make the mango relish, slice each mango on either side of the stone. Cut the flesh in these pieces into a criss-cross pattern, then push the skin inside out and slice off the flesh in neat dice. Cut the remaining mango flesh away from the stones and dice neatly.

2 Heat the oil in a saucepan, add the onion, ginger and garlic and fry gently stirring frequently, for about 5 minutes until softened but not coloured.

3 Add the mango, sugar, cayenne and a pinch of salt. Sauté for a few minutes or until the mango softens slightly. Remove from the heat, turn into a bowl and cool. Add chopped coriander, cover and chill for at least 1 hour.

4 Put the duck breasts, skin-side down, between 2 sheets of greaseproof paper and flatten them slightly by pounding with a rolling pin.

5 Remove the paper and turn the breasts skin-side up. Score the skin in a criss-cross pattern with a very sharp knife. Rub the skin all over with salt.

6 Put the duck, skin-side up, on a rack in a roasting tin. Place in a preheated oven, 200°C (400°F), Gas Mark 6 for 25 minutes, or until the duck is tender when pierced with a skewer or fork. When cooked, remove the breasts from the rack and slice thinly on the diagonal, removing the skin if preferred.

7 Arrange the slices overlapping on warmed dinner plates, with a spoonful of the chilled mango relish alongside. Garnish with coriander sprigs if liked and serve. Mangetout and new potatoes are ideal accompaniments.

Serves 6
Preparation time: 30 minutes
Cooking time: 25 minutes
Oven temperature: 200°C (400°F), Gas Mark 6

VARIATION

Duck Breasts with Raspberries

1 With a rolling pin, pound 6 duck breast fillets, skin and fat removed, between 2 sheets of greaseproof paper until flattened slightly. Rub with 2 tablespoons crushed green peppercorns.

2 Sauté duck in 2 tablespoons olive oil for 3-4 minutes on each side or until the flesh changes colour.

3 Add 200 ml/7 fl oz dry white wine, 250 g/8 oz raspberries, the grated zest and juice of 1 lime, 2 tablespoons raspberry vinegar, 2 teaspoons each clear honey and chopped fresh mint and salt and pepper to taste. Lower the heat, cover and simmer for 20 minutes, turning over once, and basting frequently with the sauce.

4 Remove duck, cover and keep warm. Strain sauce through a sieve into a saucepan. Reheat sauce.

5 Cut and serve duck as in the main recipe. Garnish with fresh raspberries and mint and serve with individual gratins dauphinois and seasonal green vegetables.

Serves 6
Preparation time: 20 minutes
Cooking time: about 30 minutes

Poussins Véronique

*'Véronique' describes dishes
which include grapes.*

2 oven-ready poussins, giblets removed
2 small lemons
4 tarragon sprigs
1 tablespoon rapeseed oil
50 g/2 oz butter
**300 ml/½ pint Chicken Stock (see
   page 8)**
1 teaspoon cornflour
2 tablespoons water
150 ml/¼ pint crème fraîche
175 g/6 oz seedless green grapes
salt and pepper
tarragon sprigs, to garnish

1 Wash the insides of the poussins, and dry them thoroughly with paper towels, then season the insides with salt and pepper to taste. Prick the lemons all over, then put 1 lemon and 2 sprigs of tarragon in the cavity of each poussin. Truss the poussins with string.

2 Heat oil and butter in a flameproof casserole large enough to hold the poussins side by side. Add 1 poussin to the casserole and cook over a moderate heat, turning frequently, for 7-10 minutes until golden. Remove and set aside. Repeat the browning with the second poussin, then return the first poussin to the casserole.

3 Pour in half the stock, cover with buttered greaseproof paper and a lid and cook over a moderate heat

for 50 minutes or until the juices from the cavities run clear when the poussins are lifted from the casserole with a fork. Turn the birds over every 10 minutes during the cooking time, first on one side, then on their breasts, then on the other side and finally on their backs.

4 Lift the poussins out of the casserole, cover tightly with foil and set aside to rest in a warm place while making the sauce.

5 Pour the remaining stock into the casserole and stir well over a moderate heat, scraping the sediment and juices from the bottom.

6 Mix the cornflour to a paste with the water, stir into the sauce and bring to the boil, stirring. Simmer, stirring, until the sauce thickens slightly. Strain into a saucepan and add crème fraîche, grapes and seasoning to taste. Heat through and keep hot over a very low heat.

7 Discard the trussing strings, cut each poussin in half lengthways and discard the lemons.

8 Arrange half a poussin on each plate, coat with sauce and garnish with fresh tarragon. Serve with any remaining sauce handed separately in a sauce boat. Serve with carrots tossed in butter and chopped mixed herbs, a seasonal green vegetable, and thinly sliced potatoes baked in the oven with onions and stock.

Serves 4
Preparation time: 20 minutes
Cooking time: about 1 hour

Chicken and Red Pesto Roulades

Red pesto, which is made from sun-dried tomatoes, pine nuts and Parmesan cheese, is more unusual than the classic green pesto made with basil, but it is now becoming more widely available in supermarkets and delicatessens. It makes an interesting alternative to tomato coulis in many dishes. If you can get purple basil for the garnish, it will complement the colours of the other ingredients.

6 large skinned chicken breast fillets
50 g/2 oz butter
4 tablespoons red pesto (see recipe introduction left)
12 back bacon rashers, rinds removed
2 tablespoons extra-virgin olive oil
125 ml/4 fl oz red wine
175 ml/6 fl oz Chicken Stock (see page 8)
4 tablespoons crème fraîche
salt and pepper

TO GARNISH:
cherry tomatoes
fresh basil leaves

1 Make a long horizontal slit through the thickest part of each chicken breast without cutting right through.
2 Beat the butter and pesto together in a bowl, then spread the mixture inside the cavities in the chicken breasts, dividing it equally between them. Close the chicken tightly around the pesto mixture.
3 Stretch the bacon rashers with the flat of a large knife blade, then wrap 2 bacon rashers tightly around each chicken breast, overlapping the rashers so that the chicken is completely enclosed in the bacon. Secure with wooden cocktail sticks.
4 Heat the oil in a large sauté pan, add the chicken breasts in a single layer and sauté over a moderate heat for 3 minutes on each side until the bacon colours.
5 Add the wine and stock and bring to the boil, spooning liquid over the chicken constantly. Cover and simmer gently for 15 minutes, or until the chicken is tender when pierced with a skewer or fork.
6 Remove the roulades from the pan with a slotted spoon, cover and keep warm. Add the crème fraîche to the pan and boil, stirring, until the liquid is thickened and reduced to a syrupy glaze. Adjust the seasoning to taste. Serve hot, with the sauce poured over and around. Garnish with cherry tomatoes and basil.

Serves 6
Preparation time: 20 minutes
Cooking time: 20-25 minutes

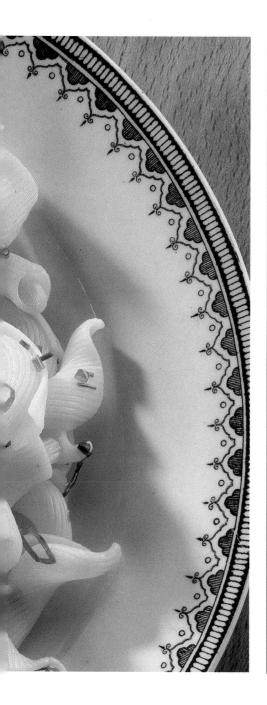

Sicilian Chicken

Everyone associates tomato sauce with Italian food, but very few expect to find a fiery hot chilli hiding in it! In fact, chillies are used quite often in Sicilian cooking, and they go surprisingly well with the other more usual Italian flavours.

2 tablespoons extra-virgin olive oil
4 skinned chicken portions
1 onion, chopped finely
1 fresh or dried red chilli, deseeded
 and chopped finely
1 garlic clove, crushed
25 g/1 oz sun-dried tomatoes in oil,
 chopped roughly

250 g/8 oz mushrooms, sliced thinly
300 ml/½ pint passata
150 ml/¼ pint dry white wine
1 teaspoon dried mixed herbs
½ teaspoon dried oregano or basil
salt and pepper

1 Heat the oil in a large flameproof casserole, add the chicken and sauté over a moderate heat for 7-10 minutes until golden on all sides. Remove with a slotted spoon and set aside on a plate.

2 Add the onion, chilli and garlic to the pan and fry, stirring frequently, for about 5 minutes until softened. Stir in the sun-dried tomatoes and mushrooms and fry for a further 5 minutes, then add the passata, white wine, herbs and salt and pepper to taste. Bring to the boil, stirring, then return the chicken to the casserole with the juices that have collected on the plate. Cover and simmer for 40 minutes or until the chicken is tender when pierced with a skewer or fork. Adjust the seasoning to taste. Serve hot, with noodles tossed in olive oil and fresh herbs.

Serves 6
Preparation time: 20 minutes
Cooking time: about 50 minutes

Pasta with Chicken, Cream and Mushroom Sauce

Use white button mushrooms for this sauce – dark ones will spoil its delicate appearance.

3 part-boned chicken breasts
1 small onion, quartered
1 carrot, chopped roughly
1 bouquet garni
a few black peppercorns
300 ml/½ pint water
2 tablespoons dry sherry (optional)
50 g/2 oz butter
250 g/8 oz button mushrooms,
sliced thinly
2 garlic cloves, crushed
1 teaspoon chopped fresh rosemary
1 tablespoon extra-virgin olive oil
375 g/12 oz dried pasta shapes
(such as farfalle, penne or fusilli)
1½ tablespoons plain flour
150 ml/¼ pint double cream
salt and pepper
fresh rosemary, to garnish

1 Put the chicken in a saucepan with the onion, carrot, bouquet garni and peppercorns. Pour in the water, and add the sherry if using.
2 Bring to the boil, then lower the heat, cover and poach the chicken for about 20 minutes until just tender when pierced with a skewer or fork.

3 Meanwhile, melt the butter in a separate saucepan, add the mushrooms, garlic, rosemary and salt and pepper to taste, and sauté over a moderate heat, stirring frequently, for about 5 minutes until the juices run. Remove from the heat. With a slotted spoon, transfer the mushrooms from the buttery liquid to a bowl.
4 Bring a large saucepan of water to the boil, swirl in the oil and add ½ teaspoon salt. Add the pasta and boil, uncovered, over a moderate heat for 10 minutes, or according to packet instructions, until *al dente*.
5 Meanwhile, lift the chicken out of the poaching liquid, then strain the liquid into a jug. Cut the chicken into strips, discarding the skin and bones.

6 Return the mushroom cooking liquid to the heat, sprinkle in the flour and cook for 1-2 minutes, stirring. Add the chicken poaching liquid a little at a time, beating vigorously after each addition.
7 Bring to the boil, stirring. Lower the heat and add chicken, mushrooms, cream and seasoning. Stir well, then simmer, stirring frequently, for 5 minutes until thickened.
8 Drain the pasta and turn into a warmed serving bowl. Pour in the sauce and toss to mix with the pasta. Serve garnished with rosemary.

Serves 4
Preparation time: 30 minutes
Cooking time: 30 minutes

Chicken with 40 Garlic Cloves

A traditional Provençal dish – perfect for a Sunday lunch 'al fresco'.

1 x 2 kg/4 lb oven-ready chicken,
   giblets removed
1 bouquet garni
4 tablespoons extra-virgin olive oil
40 garlic cloves, separated but
   not peeled
1 celery stick, chopped
salt and pepper
a few sprigs each of rosemary, sage
   and thyme, to garnish

FOR SEALING:

4 tablespoons plain flour
4 teaspoons water

1 Wash and dry chicken cavity, insert bouquet garni and season to taste. Truss the chicken with string.
2 Heat the oil in a large flameproof casserole into which the bird just fits. Add the garlic and celery, then the chicken and cook until it is lightly coloured on all sides.
3 Cover the casserole with its lid. Make a paste with the flour and water and seal around the edge.
4 Place in a preheated oven 180°C (350°F), Gas Mark 4 for 2-2¼ hours, without opening the oven door.
5 Break the flour and water seal, then lift out the chicken and place on a warmed serving platter. Arrange the garlic cloves around the chicken and garnish with sprigs of rosemary, sage and thyme. Serve hot, with mashed potatoes and a juicy vegetable dish such as ratatouille.

Serves 4
Preparation time: 15 minutes
Cooking time: 2-2¼ hours
Oven temperature: 180°C (350°F),
Gas Mark 4

Traditional Christmas Roast Turkey

Consult the chart on page 4 for correct cooking times for different weights. Adjust the quantity of stuffing accordingly. Cook extra stuffing in the oven for the last 30 minutes of roasting time. For ease of carving, you could also bone the turkey (see page 7), stuff and roll it.

1 x 5-6 kg/10-12 lb oven-ready turkey, dressed weight with giblets removed
1 apple, cored and quartered
1 onion, quartered
chestnut stuffing (see at right)
50 g/2 oz unsalted butter, softened
6-8 streaky bacon rashers
salt and pepper
holly sprigs, to garnish

1 Wash the inside of the turkey and dry thoroughly with paper towels. Put the apple and onion quarters inside the cavity and season to taste.
2 Pack the chestnut stuffing loosely into the neck of the bird (if packed too tightly, heat will not penetrate the centre of the bird). Truss the bird, then weigh and calculate the cooking time according to the chart (see page 4).
3 Put the turkey on a large sheet of strong foil and transfer to a large roasting tin into which the bird just fits. Brush the bird all over with softened butter, arrange bacon rashers over the breast and legs, and sprinkle with pepper to taste. Close the foil around the bird to make a loose parcel.
4 Roast in a preheated oven, 190°C (375°F), Gas Mark 5 for the calculated cooking time. Open the foil and remove the bacon 30 minutes before the end, and baste the turkey with the cooking juices to allow the skin to become crisp and golden brown. To test if the turkey is cooked, pierce the thickest part of a thigh with a skewer or fork – the juices should run clear.
5 Lift the turkey out of the tin, cover tightly with clean foil and set aside to rest in a warm place for 30 minutes. Meanwhile, make the gravy (see at right).
6 Discard the trussing string. Put the turkey on a warmed serving platter and garnish with holly sprigs. Serve with Brussels sprouts, roast and creamed potatoes and bacon and chipolata rolls. Bread sauce, cranberry jelly or sauce, and the gravy are served separately.

Serves 8-10
Preparation time: about 1 hour
Cooking time: about 4 hours, according to size
Oven temperature: 190°C (375°F), Gas Mark 5

ACCOMPANIMENTS

Chestnut Stuffing

125 g/4 oz streaky bacon rashers, rinds removed, chopped
3 celery sticks, chopped finely
1 onion, chopped finely
175 g/6 oz canned unsweetened chestnuts, drained and chopped finely
175 g/6 oz fresh breadcrumbs (white or wholemeal, according to taste)
finely grated zest and juice of 1 lemon
finely grated zest and juice of 1 orange
1 egg, beaten
1 tablespoon chopped fresh sage or 1½ teaspoons dried
salt and freshly ground black pepper

1 Gently fry the bacon until the fat runs. Add celery and onion, and fry for 5 minutes. Turn into a bowl, and mix in the remaining ingredients.

Gravy

1 Pour off all the fat from the roasting tin, leaving about 3 tablespoons of the cooking juices. Set the tin on top of the stove, sprinkle in 2 tablespoons plain flour and cook gently, stirring, for 1-2 minutes until golden.
2 Stir in 450 ml/¾ pint Giblet Stock (see page 9) and bring to the boil, stirring. Stir in 4 tablespoons red wine or sherry, a pinch of dried sage and salt and pepper to taste. Simmer until thickened

Balti chicken 98
biryani, chicken 95
boning 9
brick, chicken in a 54

Cajun blackened chicken 78
cannelloni, chicken 43
Champagne, chicken with
    cream sauce and 110
cheese: chicken with white
    wine, Gruyère and
    mushrooms 117
    chicken with garlic, herbs
    and cream cheese 31
chestnut stuffing 126
chilli chicken 16
Chinese sweet and sour
    chicken 90
chop suey 37
chow mein 53
chowder, chicken and
    sweetcorn 59
Circassian chicken 74
club sandwich 49
coq au vin 68
Cordon Bleu, chicken 105
Coronation chicken 56
couscous, chicken 70
cream cheese, chicken with
    garlic, herbs and 31
croquettes, chicken and
    lemon 45
croûte, chicken breasts en 112
curries: chicken with chick
    peas and potatoes 100
    Indonesian chicken and
    coconut 86

Devilled spatchcocked
    poussins 24
dhansak, chicken 100
drumsticks, barbecued 18
duck: duck breasts with
    raspberries and lime 118

duck breasts with spicy
    mango relish 118
duck terrine en croûte 115
duck terrine with
    cherries 115
Peking duck 91
quick stir-fried duck with
    pineapple 34
roast duck with fresh orange
    and Cointreau sauce 113
soy duck 36

Five-spice chicken 34
French roast chicken 38

Garlic cloves, chicken with
    40 125
giblet stock 8
gravy 126
gumbo, chicken and smoked
    ham 76

Jalfrezi, chicken 99
Jamaican jerk chicken 81
jambalaya 79
jerk chicken, Oliver's 81
jointing 8-9

Kebabs, chicken and sweet
    pepper 15
Kiev, chicken 116
korma, chicken 94

Lemon chicken 20

Malaysian chicken noodle
    and prawn stew 84
Malaysian chicken stew with
    spinach and crab 84
mangetout and chicken in
    black bean sauce 32
Marengo, chicken 60
mushrooms: chicken with
    oyster mushrooms 102

Nasi goreng 82
Normandy chicken 108

Paella, Spanish 67.
pan-fried chicken breasts 26
paprikash, chicken 26
pasta with chicken, cream and
    mushroom sauce 124
pasticciata, chicken 43
pâté, chicken liver 21
Peking duck 91
penne with chicken and
    pesto 33
peppers, chicken suprêmes
    with roast 107
Persian chicken 73
pesto, chicken and red 121
pies: chicken pot pie 51
    old English chicken and
    vegetable pie 51
pollo alla cacciatora 65
pollo alla Valdostana 66
pollo tonnato 63
poulet bonne femme 57
poussins Véronique 120

Risotto, chicken liver 46
roulade, chicken and red
    pesto 121

St Clement's chicken 73
salads: chicken and grape 23
    chicken, red pepper and
    lemon 12
    smoked chicken, orange
    and avocado 23
    Thai chicken and
    papaya 83
    warm chicken liver 29
satay, chicken 89
sauté of chicken 10
Sicilian chicken 123
soups: chicken and sweet
    corn chowder 59

hot and sour chicken 87
turkey and chestnut 59
turkey and vegetable 52
waterzooi 41
Spanish paella 67
spiced roast chicken 109
stock 7-8
Sunday roast chicken 44
Swiss chicken 31

Tagine, Moroccan 71
tandoori chicken 97
Tex-Mex chicken with salsa
    28
Thai chicken and papaya
    salad 83
tikka, chicken 97
tikka masala, chicken 92
turkey: Christmas turkey and
    vegetable soup 52
    curried turkey meatballs 40
    Italian pot-roast turkey 62
    sautéed with Marsala 17
    stir-fried with pine nuts 13
    traditional Christmas roast
    turkey 126
    turkey and chestnut soup 59
    turkey in a brick 54
    turkey mole 75
    turkey satay 89
    turkey tetrazzini 48

Vegetable terrine with chicken
    mousseline 104

Waldorf, chicken 25
waterzooi 41
wine: chicken with white wine,
    cream and tarragon 110
    chicken with white wine,
    Gruyère and
    mushrooms 117

Yakitori chicken 15